THE BENGAL TIGRESS

Abhijit Naskar is one of twenty-first century's most influential minds in Neuroscience and an untiring advocate of global harmony and peace. He became a beloved best-selling author all over the world with his very first book "The Art of Neuroscience in Everything", that heralded the advent of a beautiful scientific philosophy. With various of his pioneering ventures into the Neuropsychology of religious sentiments, he has hugely contributed to humanity's attempt of diminishing religious differences, for which he is popularly hailed as a humanitarian who incessantly works towards taking the human civilization in the path of sweet general harmony.

THE
BENGAL
TIGRESS

A TREATISE ON GENDER
EQUALITY

ABHIJIT
NASKAR

The Bengal Tigress: A Treatise on Gender Equality

Copyright © 2017 Abhijit Naskar

This is a work of non-fiction

An Amazon Publishing Company, 1st Edition, 2017

Printed in United States of America

ISBN-13: 978-1545322680

DEDICATION

To every form of femininity,

the mother,

the sister,

the wife,

the friend,

and the colleague.

CONTENTS

CHAPTER 1
Introduction

What is an "ideal woman"? What are the characteristics that this phrase reflects? What is the nature of the "ideal feminine"? Are you thinking about the answers to these perplexing questions right this very moment! Are you! Okay, stop thinking right now. A rational mind of the thinking society should not even be considering such obsolete questions that depict women as some sort of alienated creatures, that require constant labeling. Instead, you should be thinking, who the heck is greater than the women to define them as "ideal"!

As it happens, the image of an "ideal woman" is constructed by the male psyche, out of an evolutionary urge for undisputed authority over the society, and thereafter nourished by the entire human society, male and female alike. I am pain-stricken to say that, today all that remains, is a fabricated image of an "ideal woman", which, every woman fights till death to attain, and every man perceives as a measure of femininity. When such fabrication replaces the real thing with its unrealistic shine, humanity

3

inadvertently loses its right to the title "Sapiens" or "Wise". Any woman who is brave enough to defy that delusional image and build her own identity, however she deems best, is the tigress that I revere. That tigress lies deep within the subconscious of every woman. All you have to do is bring it up to the surface and manifest it through your actions. Become endowed with such bravery that even if the whole world deems you worthless, it does not diminish the slightest bit of your respect for the self.

You my Sister, are the woman, who has the power within you to mend the society's perception of what a woman really is. O my Courageous Sister! You have to become the beacon of hope for all women around you and then for the whole society. You are your own measure. And that measure shall become the measure of femininity in the whole world. Remember though, feminism is not the quality I am talking about, for the term itself has become too congested with political ideologies, hence, the quality I am talking about is plain everyday humanism, with a special tinge of femininity.

The feminine power can add special characteristic aspects to Humanism, more than any masculinity in the world. The female brain itself is a highly intuitive emotion-processing machine, which when put to practice in the progress of the society, would do much more than any man can with all his analytical perspectives. What a hundred caring, courageous and conscientious women can achieve in ten years, would take a thousand men a hundred years. A handful of brave tigresses, fortified with the power of will, can take the society to such heights of advancement, that it will become a standard of progress for thousands of generations yet to come.

For thousands of years, the dumb, uncivilized, stone-age society has reduced women to mere prizes to be won, objects to be shown off, and playthings to be abused and toyed with. Now is the time to stop this primitive madness. And I am afraid, the initiation for the elimination of the society's patriarchal biases shall not come from the male masses, it can only rise from the heart of the woman - from the deepest fathoms of the individual feminine self. It all begins with you, O Bold One!

And if attempting to make the world a civilized one, makes you a bad woman in the eyes of the dumb patriarchal society, then, by all means, be it. The world doesn't need a good woman who is meekly obedient to the uncivilized social norms that advocate female inferiority. The world needs those bad women who can think for themselves, to break the primeval norms of the society that consistently drag the human civilization back to the stone-age. You are not born to follow the society, you are born to inspire it - you are born to teach it - you are born to build it.

Humanity has had so many teachers in the form of thinkers, yet it has not stopped fighting within itself. Most of these teachers have been men. It's time, that teachers have to rise from the feminine part of the society - it's time that thinkers have to rise from the depths of the female psyche. I am a scientist who studies the human mind, including the sexual differences in mental faculties, and I am telling you, ten female thinkers can teach humanity lessons equivalent to the teachings of a hundred male thinkers of history.

Arise my Sister! Awake my Sister! Start walking in the path of building your own identity! Start walking in the path of becoming an ideal for your society! Remember, ideal is the one, who knows the self. So, recognize the self first, and then start walking in the path of becoming a glorious sun shining over whole humanity!

CHAPTER 2
The Feminine Power

Any nation that does not learn to place women on the same pedestal of respect and dignity as men, will never in a thousand years attain greatness. How dare a person tell a woman, how to dress, how to talk, how to behave! Any being who does that, is no human. The society that does not hail women as equal of man, in all aspects of life, can never progress. Man and Woman, are the two wheels of the society. Both of them must keep rolling for the society to move forward.

Any doctrine that advocates superiority of one gender over the other, must be discarded at once. Any book that spreads weakness in the heart of one gender, and authoritarianism in the other, must be burnt to ashes. Any institution that teaches one gender to be subservient to the other, must be demolished for good. Any force that is not concerned with the equal progress of all humans of the society, regardless of race, religion and gender, has no earthly right to exist.

And the major cause for the degeneration of the human race is this - it is that there are more forces in the world to enforce male superiority, in the name of religion, intellect or progress, than there are to obliterate such barbarianism and enforce gender-blind humanism. Being gender-blind does not mean not recognizing the gender of a person, it simply means not to give in to the primordial evil of gender bias.

However, biology without bias is nonexistent. The human brain constructs various biases to suit the individual's survival needs. But it is the civilized conscience that has to decide whether or not to act upon certain biases. For example, driven the brain's libidinal circuitry a young man's penis is evolutionarily biased towards any beautiful woman, regardless of whether the man is already in a relationship or not. Here, if the man gives in to his primeval urges, he would simply make a perfect specimen of a penis-driven caveman.

But, over millions of years the human brain has developed faculties of self-control to keep such primeval responses and biases tamed and not manifest through behavior. This is the sign of a civilized conscience. The moment when humanity learns to tame all its primeval biases, only then it will be worth the title "Sapiens", not any earlier. Right now, we are only a developing species, learning to take bold steps towards genuine progress.

We are a young species. And we have a lot to learn. Also, we have a lot to unlearn - I am talking about our primeval traits such as promiscuity, supernaturalism, misogyny, authoritarianism and fundamentalism. It will take some time to unlearn all these evil traits of the beastly part of the mind, and develop civilized values on top of them, but the efforts begin now.

We no longer have any time to waste, entertaining our dark side. It is time we recognize those evil elements of our internal world and start working untiringly on eradicating them. And how are we going to do that? How are we going to diminish this internal darkness of the mind? Darkness is merely the absence of light. And it is time, that we replace the darkness within with light - replace ignorance with knowledge - replace weakness with strength - replace prejudice with reasoning - replace hatred with love - replace sectarianism with assimilation - replace discrimination with acceptance.

Remember, for a society to truly progress we don't need woman or man, we need a fully-fledged human - nothing short of that would do. In the progressive society of thinking humanity, gender equality is not something you believe in, it is a quintessential part of human existence. Do not forget my friend, the future of human civilization is predicated on the quality of human existence, not just the quality of male existence. I am saying again, gender equality is not a belief, it is not an idea - it is a key element of the society that will define whether we the humans shall march ahead towards glory and advancement, or sink into the abyss of an existential doom.

Women are no sheep. Women are no fragile showpiece to be placed above the fire-place. Women of the thinking society are the builders of nations. Women of the sentient society are the builders of the world. And given the same honor and dignity as men, women can build a much better and more harmonious world. Harmony and conflict-solving run in their veins. Whereas men have evolved into more authoritarian creatures.

All the bloodsheds in human history have been caused by men, not women. And there is a biological reason for this. As boys grow up to become men, their testosterone becomes a major driving force behind their innate urge to have authority over their environment. Aggression and rage both serve as crucial emotional and behavioral expressions to satisfy that need for authority. The female brain, is engineered by Mother Nature to avoid conflicts at all cost, whereas the male brain pleasures conflicts in the purpose of having authority. Women are motivated on a molecular level to ease and even prevent social conflicts. Maintaining an inter-personal relationship at all costs is the female brain's primary goal. The female brain has a far more negative alert reaction to relationship conflict and rejection than does the male brain. Men often relish interpersonal conflict and competition. They even get a positive psychological boost from it. In women, conflict is more likely to set in motion a cascade of negative neurochemical reactions, creating feelings of stress and fear. Just the thought of a possible imminent conflict can be read by the female brain as a threat to the relationship and hence can give rise to serious concerns. That's why women are neurologically more capable of keeping their rage in control than men, so that it doesn't hamper any of their interpersonal relationships in the society.

Studies have shown that though men and women say that they feel anger for an equal number of minutes per day, men get physically aggressive twenty times more often than women. Due to the abundance of testosterone receptors in the amygdala, high testosterone level makes it even more difficult for a man to tame his rage and aggression. Other than testosterone, a man's brain circuit for aggression is highly influenced by vasopressin, cortisol and adrenalin. And actually in most cases when a man's anger reaches the boiling point, it gives him an utter sensation of pleasure. The pleasure of utter aggression further motivates a man to win the fight.

All these are evolutionarily encoded inside the male brain to ensure the survival of the progeny and mate at all costs. But in today's world, this male trait ends up doing more harm than good. The neurologically encoded primitive instinct of aggression, rising from the amygdala, often finds its way out in modern situations and quite unconsciously compels the men to act as if they are in the environment of the wild.

In an adult human brain, the male amygdala is significantly larger than the female amygdala, even when total brain size is taken into consideration. While on the contrary women have slightly larger prefrontal cortex and anterior cingulate cortex that are involved in controlling the rage and avoiding any kind of conflict. As a result, women in general have better hold of their anger response than men. All men either consciously or subconsciously crave for authority over their environment, especially over their peers in the society, male and female alike. Women on the other hand, crave for intimacy especially from their female peers in the society. Colloquially this is what you call "gossiping".

Now one might wonder, why do women spend so much time in talking to their female peers? The answer can again be found in the process of biological evolution of the human mind. Just like the evolutionary expression of aggression in men, gossiping is an evolutionary feature of the female psychology. Women trade various secrets from their personal experiences through gossiping in order to create connection and intimacy with their female peers. By doing this, what they are accomplishing is the development of close-knit cliques with secret rules. In these new groups, talking, telling secrets, and gossiping, in fact, often become women's favorite activities - their tools to navigate and ease the ups and downs and stresses of life.

Connecting through talking activates the pleasure centers in a girl's brain. Here I'm not talking about a small amount of pleasure. This is huge. It's a major dopamine and oxytocin rush, which is the biggest, fattest and extremely substantial neurological reward you can get outside of an orgasm. Dopamine stimulates the motivation and pleasure circuits in the brain, while Oxytocin triggers a sense of intimacy. The combination of dopamine and oxytocin forms the biological basis of the female drive for intimacy with its stress-reducing effect.

Thus, women are driven by a desire for connection with their peers in the society. Their dopamine and oxytocin rush from talking and connecting keeps them motivated to seek out these intimate connections. But this is typically a girl thing – an exclusive reality of the female mental universe. Now imagine, what happens when you put such a fantastic trait into practice in the pursuit of resolving the giant conflicts of the society. That's the best thing that can ever happen to this world. Evolutionarily speaking, conflict-resolution is a fundamental mental faculty of women, way beyond the wildest imaginations of any man. Replace all male leaders of the world with vigorous, caring and conscientious female leaders, and they will turn this world into a genuine abode of peace in a few decades.

Women are not playthings to be toyed with - they are the best leaders, thinkers and teachers that the world can ever have. And this is not some sort of big talk by a feminist, this is a scientist talking, standing on the bed-rock of neurobiology. I am no feminist. Even though the term "feminism" is founded upon the basic principle of gender equality, it possesses its own fundamental gender bias, which makes it inclined towards the wellbeing of women, over the wellbeing of the whole society. And if history has shown anything, it is that such fundamental biases in time corrupt even the most glorious ideas and give birth to prejudice, bigotry and differentiation.

Psychologically speaking, devotion to one gender often brings along callousness towards the other gender. Hence, right now, Feminism may seem to be a glorious notion which deserves all the commendation in the world, but it is psychologically destined to turn into an evil authoritarian ideology, if not properly aligned with the wellbeing of the whole society, rather than just one gender.

Any idea of differentiation is bondage. True liberation lies in the assimilation of all. And Feminism, despite being deemed as advocacy of gender equality, is like an aneurysm in the social psyche, which is waiting to go boom, sooner or later. And when it does, the human population shall have to face yet another primeval blood-feud between the two sides of sexism. Hence, true liberation of the society lies not in Feminism, it lies in Humanism - it lies in diminishing all the evil discriminations in the world - it lies in the genuine concern for the wellbeing of every human being.

We have been fighting over race, religion, and creeds for ages. Now is the time to stop these barbarian fights - not to begin yet another fight to protect the vanity of a sophisticated term. I am not saying, Feminism is evil. It is too humane to be disgraced with the adjective "evil".

But this "humane" is inclined towards one gender, and that's where the problem festers.

The general human brain always craves for meaning in everything around it, in every phenomenon, in every idea, in every term. Every term or idea elicits certain implicit or explicit emotional responses in the perceiver's mind. And, feminism is no different. The very first notion that the brain concocts in an effort to explain Feminism, is that it has something to do with the "Feminine" - that it has something to do with women.

The very gender bias of the term quite unavoidable elicits an implicit emotional response in the human mind, which consists of affectionate elements towards the feminine and aversive elements towards the masculine. Thus, despite being not an anti-male term, feminism quite unintentionally evokes an implicit, or simply subconscious, anti-male response in the perceiver's mind, which over time gets stronger, until it becomes so strong that it turns into an explicit emotional response and manifests through anti-male behavior. Thus, feminism glitters with a fundamental psychological element of differentiation – it fosters a "us versus them" sentiment. And that my friend, is a major cause for concern, the same as my concern for the term "mankind".

Often the term "mankind" is quite gloriously used in the English language to refer to the whole of humanity. Here humanity is defined by the dominant characteristics of men, which again quite inadvertently undermines the existential significance of women. Hence, the only word that should be used in all circumstances while referring to our entire species is "humanity" or "humankind, instead of "mankind". And, it is "humanism" that should run in the veins of the thinking humanity, not a certain gender-oriented "ism". This entire book is a treatise on gender equality, and as such, it may be hailed as a work of feminism, but it is not - it is a work of humanism.

O Brave Sister, no one is going to come to you and say "lead me, for I have gone astray"! You need to raise yourself as a human being and become a glorious figure of valor. You are meant to figure out the edges of human excellence and build the map which will guide the others in their endeavors of life. And all of this can only be achieved driven, not by feminism, but by the innate force of humanism. Humanism is not a pompous philosophy to be talked and debated about by a handful of intellectuals - it is the purest form of moral compass, which defines the civilized heart of thinking humanity. It is not a luxury, rather an evolutionary necessity, if we are to keep evolving in the path of further mental and physical advancement, beyond the limitations imposed by the primitive ignorance of our wild past.

In the society of thinking humanity, you are first a human, then everything else. Which means, to a real human, humanism takes preference over everything else, - to the conscientious human humanism takes preference over gender, race, religion or anything else. And this is no sophisticated philosophy of the intellectuals. When you hail the very foundation of all human characteristics as a philosophy, the subconscious part of the mind begins to incorporate various complex cognitive supplementary elements to define that philosophy, in the line of other philosophical ideas, and in the process, the term "humanism" loses its plain ordinary everyday closeness. Somehow, the term philosophy, when used adjacent to the term Humanism, makes it less innately human and more conceptual. Humanism is not a concept. It is the very core of the global heart of humanity. It is the backbone – the bed-rock – the foundation upon which the global edifice of conscientious humanity is being built.

We the humans do not deem the "phenomenon of love" as a philosophy, rather we quite elementarily embrace it as the most natural part of human existence. And humanism is the purest form of love that can ever exist throughout the lifetime of a species. Humanism means loving all humans as your own family beyond the man-made citadels of separations. Remember, any notion of separation is bondage. And liberation comes through breaking down the primitive, prejudicial barriers that separate you from your fellow humans on the basis of belief, gender, color, ethnicity or anything else.

CHAPTER 3

Objectification of Women

I cannot believe, that I, a member of a species, which takes pride in its wisdom, am saying "women are humans too, not objects"! What is the reason for such a misfortune to have befallen the human society? In the primitive days, aggression of our forefathers played the most crucial role in the survival of themselves, their mates and their progeny. Eventually, they became the guiding figures of their environment. Thus, the human society evolved into a patriarchal society, in which the major role of the women was, and still mostly remains homemaking and domestic chores.

But evolution is a relentless process, it never stops. A species that does not evolve, is destined by the law of nature to get extinct. And in this process of evolution, the species often has to take some revolutionary steps that define whether it shall keep on living or get extinct. The evolutionary history of humans is filled with many such revolutionary footsteps.

For example, the dietary shift of our ancestral species Homo habilis from a vegetarian fruit-enriched diet to a non-vegetarian diet of scavenged meat set in motion a tripling of their brain volume. A vegetarian diet does indeed have health benefits, but if our ancestors had only lived on vegetables and had never touched meat, we would've never become the smartest species on earth. Morally it may be better to not kill any creature for their flesh, but biologically, meat was one of the greatest factors involved in the rise of the psychology of thinking humanity. Thus, this revolutionary dietary shift provided a great push towards the evolution of modern human consciousness.

The next big evolutionary leap came from our ancestral species named Homo erectus. They solved one of the most important pieces of human evolutionary puzzle - the mystery of fire. Every animal on earth that had ever encountered fire, had run away from it. If Homo erectus could do the unimaginable and conquer their instinctive fear, they'd harness a new power. They just needed the nerve to reach into the blaze, and they did. The impact of fire was an enormous step forward in human evolution.

Right now, we have reached yet another crossroads of human evolution. And the step we take now shall define our future. Now is the time, that we have to make a decision. We have to decide whether we shall hang on to our barbarian prejudices like cave-people, or we shall tear those primitive shackles apart into pieces and move forward like real civilized humans. Now is the time that we make conscientious efforts towards becoming a real wise species, free from all sorts of bigotry, mysticism and sectarianism. And such a tremendous evolutionary mission can only be accomplished through reasoning - it can only be accomplished through knowledge. Knowledge shall set the mind free.

A quintessential part of this liberation is gender egalitarianism. Humanity cannot be liberated with its feet stuck deep into the garbage of gender discrimination or misogyny. And the first step towards achieving that egalitarian society, is to accept women in our hearts for what they really are, not what the society has turned them into. And this, I am not saying to a man or a woman – I am saying this to the human in you.

The representation of women in the society, especially through mass media has been the most delusional act ever done on the grounds of human existence. It has, throughout the years, reduced women to nothing more than prizes to be won, centerpieces to be shown off, and playthings to be abused. Moreover, it has cooked up and fed the masses a false definition of beauty. Naturally sociological pressure compels the women to compare themselves to that false definition of beauty. And the men feel psychologically driven by social cues to compare the women in their lives to what they see on television screens, in magazines, and on billboards.

In this whole delusional process of objectification of the feminine both the human self, be it man or woman, and the society have lost the cognitive ability to perceive and realize the true nature of femininity. Remember, a society where feminine beauty is defined not by the human self on genuine intellectual and sentimental grounds, but by a computer software on the grounds of economic interest, is more dead than alive. It is a society of human bodies, not human beings.

Because of the delusional beauty put forth by the media and accepted at large by the patriarchal society we have seen explosive increases in plastic surgery and an overwhelming occurrence of eating disorders. The harsh reality of this so-called smart world is that when a woman gazes at an airbrushed beauty wishing for the model's thighs or slender hips she fails to register that the image she sees before her has nothing to do with reality. The images on television, on youtube, on magazines or on billboards are all mere fabrications, that are carefully designed by graphic artists commissioned to change appearance and stimulate desire. Each image is painstakingly worked over. Teeth and eyeballs are bleached white - blemishes, wrinkles and stray hairs are airbrushed away.

According to a New York retoucher, *"Almost every photograph you see for a national advertiser these days has been worked on by a retoucher to some degree... Fundamentally, our job is to correct the basic deficiencies in the original photograph or, in effect, to improve upon the appearance of reality"*.

In some cases, a picture is not even of one woman, rather an amalgamation of body parts of several different models – a mouth from this one, arms from that one and legs from a third. Basically, by inviting women to compare their own real image with the airbrushed perfection of the media, advertising erodes self-esteem, then offers to sell it back, for a price. And this expensive illusory perfection leads women down a road of destructive self-comparison which one way or another ends up in self-immolation.

A 30 years old woman originally from Upstate NY, who now resides in Canada, is one of the millions who have fallen victim to the delusional perfection presented in the media. Hence, she has spent considerable time trying to match up to the fake standard. She says,

"My eating disorder started my senior year of high school. I remember reading teen magazines as a young girl and wanting to look like those girls, but I had not a clue how to achieve that goal. At 17, what started out as a friendly competition with a friend turned into something else. At first she lost more weight than me, but after my first real heartbreak and High School graduation and starting college, I felt that controlling my eating was the only way I could have any control.

What started out as exercise and a healthy diet turned into obsessive workout and calorie counting, until I lost control and became bulimic for about a year. I also had breast implants when I was 19. Mine were unusually small, so on top of feeling I lacked femininity, I also felt like a freak. My doctor gave me larger implants than I had asked for, which led to me being treated like a ditz for 10 years."

Years later, at 5'7" and 130 pounds, she still finds herself struggling with her body image.

"I think about my weight constantly. I always wish to be just a little bit smaller. I would say at

least three to five solid hours of my day are me
thinking about food, my weight, how I"m going
to lose more, and how I am going to keep it off."

Her battle is ongoing and has lasted for over 15 years, but she is far from alone. The longing she felt looking at slim images in beauty magazines or on the television is spreading exponentially among girls, especially during adolescence, like a plague.

Negative body image in adolescent girls is of growing concern in the modern society. As girls go through puberty, their bodies gain adipose and move farther away from the thin childish appearance. You simply need to take a look at a fashion magazine to see how the fake ideal feminine body represented in it is often asexual and childlike. Such a medium influences the girls and causes them to become dissatisfied with their natural appearance. And this leads to depression. Importantly, depression is a significant risk factor for substance abuse and suicide attempts.

Listen my dear sister! You only fix something, when it's broken. And you - are far from broken.

Say to yourself, *I am perfect, the way I am*. Say to yourself, *I am beautiful the way I am*. Say to yourself, *those who do not accept me the way I am, do not deserve me in their life*. You are who you are, because of all your unique physiological and psychological traits. And the moment, you try overwhelming these uniquely "you" traits with the fake traits shown on TV, you essentially lose the "youness". Hence, you cease to exist as a real thinking human being. All that remains is a robot run by the fake shadow of perfection.

Here, what you need to know is that beauty is an illusion, created by Mother Nature to drive the human species in the path of reproduction. In reality, beauty is irrelevant to human life, especially in a relationship. What you today perceive as beautiful and special, over time, becomes not so special. That's how the human brain works. It is not beauty that keeps a relationship alive, it is attachment. Without attachment, a naked body is merely a lifeless sex toy.

A man who wakes up to a pair of double D breasts of his wife every morning, is neurologically destined to get used to them, regardless of their size. This is called "Habituation". But this process of habituation does not say anything about the love and care between two persons in a committed relationship.

Love is not the primeval surge of libidinal lust that a person receives when meeting a suitable partner for the first time. Love in the truest sense of the term is born much later in a relationship, when both sides get to the know the truest selves of each other. And when love is born out of the pyre of commitment and attachment, it is no longer about having sex, it is about making love and becoming one with each other in every manner possible. Remember, you can have sex even with a complete stranger, but it is the other half of your soul, that you make love with. And this love, is not definable in any manner by the size of the breasts or the length of the penis, rather it is defined by whether or not you can see yourself in your partner's eyes. Lust is defined by the size of private parts, but love is defined by the glorious blend of sentiments and values.

Now let's investigate the underlying neurobiology of this glorious fusion of mental elements, called Love. In the very early days of a relationship it is not really love, what we feel, rather it is a sensation of attraction which is subconsciously driven by libido. Love begins with this stage of primitive lust and attraction. The bodily characteristics of a person, poke the level of sex hormones (testosterone and estrogen) and pheromones. Lust is initiated at this stage through the physical attraction and flirting. This is an evolutionary behavior of humankind that biologically enables a human to find a healthy, fertile and suitable mate.

Following the cue of lust, the major attraction symptoms kick in, which are usually known as the symptoms of love, such as sweaty palms, tremors in the whole body, restlessness, loss of appetite and sleep, thumping heart, butterflies in the stomach etc. Such symptoms occur because the body is flooded with neurochemicals like Dopamine, Norepinephrine, and Phenylethylamine (PEA). It is only when this euphoria wears off, that the ultimate and deepest stage of love prevails that is the attachment phenomenon. And the chemicals that make this possible are Oxytocin, Vasopressin and Endorphins.

As time goes by, the crazy love sensation diminishes and the feeling of closeness and attachment grows and thereafter prevails till the last breath of life.

Research has shown that due to this primitive programming it takes the male brain only one fifth of a second to classify a woman as sexually hot or not. The unconscious mind reaches to the conclusion long before a man's conscious mind engages in the process.

For men and women, the initial calculations about romance are totally unconscious, and they're very different. Men are chasers and women are choosers. It's our inheritance from the primitive ancestors who learned, over millions of years, how to propagate their genes.

Darwin noted, males of all species are made for wooing females, and females typically choose among their suitors. This is the brain architecture of love, engineered by the reproductive winners in evolution. Even the shapes, faces, smells, and ages of the mates we choose are influenced by patterns set ages ago.

Falling in love is one of the most irrational behaviors or brain states imaginable for both men and women. The brain becomes "illogical" in the throes of new romance. If we could travel along a person's brain circuits as he or she is falling in love, we'd begin in an area deep at the center of the brain called the ventral tegmental area (VTA). We'd see the cells in this area rapidly producing dopamine.

Dopamine is the brain's feel-good neurotransmitter for motivation and reward. As the brain gets filled with dopamine, the person starts to feel a pleasant buzz. The flood of dopamine stimulates the nucleus accumbens (NAc), the brain region involved in the feeling of pleasure and reward, or simply the brain's reward center.

In a male brain, we'd see the dopamine being mixed with testosterone and vasopressin, while in a female brain, it gets mixed with estrogen and oxytocin. The fusion of dopamine with these other hormones makes an addictive impact over the person, leaving both the male and female exhilarated and head over heels in love.

And the last stand of this mad love is the caudate nucleus (CN), the area for memorizing the look and identity of whoever is giving pleasure. Here we'd see all the minuscule details about the woman or the man being indelibly chiseled into the permanent memory. At this point your beloved one becomes literally unforgettable. Once the train of love has made these three stops at the VTA, NAc and CN, we'd see the brain's lust and love circuits merge together as they focus only on the beloved one.

The brain circuits for passionately being in love or the so-called infatuation-love share brain circuits with states of obsession, mania, intoxication, thirst, and hunger. Also, as I mentioned earlier the brain circuits that are activated when we are in love match those of the drug addict desperately craving for the next fix. The most remarkable data on the neurobiological foundation of romantic love come from the studies conducted by Bartels and Zeki (2000),

Aron et al. (2005, 2011), Xu et al. (2010), and Ortigue et al. (2007).

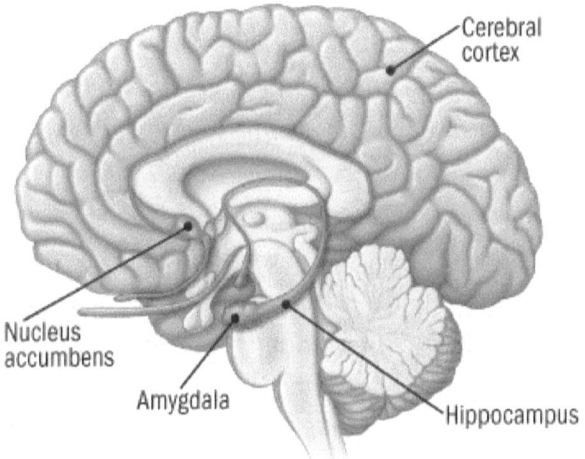

Figure 3.1 Nucleus accumbens, Amygdala, Hippocampus and Cortex

The amygdala (fear-alert system) and the prefrontal cortex (judgment and critical thinking system) are turned way down when the love circuits are running at their full potential. This is why we become literally blind to the shortcomings of our dearly beloved. The same thing happens when people take Ecstasy. So romantic love is a natural way of getting high. The classic symptoms of early love are also similar to the initial effects of drugs such as cocaine, heroin and morphine. Narcotics trigger the brain's reward circuit, causing effects similar to romance. Hence the well-known phrase "addicted to love" is scientifically quite literal and accurate. Studies have shown that this early ecstatic stage of romantic love lasts for around six to eight months. During this stage break-up can be catastrophic leading to withdrawal like symptoms, as the body keeps hankering for the sensation of euphoria connected to the person. These early months of a relationship, romantically involved partners literally crave for each other and feel undeniably dependent on each other. This is such an extreme state that the partner's well-being becomes more important than one's own.

- *Love Sutra: The Neuroscientific Manual of Love*

After the euphoria of the mad love phase wears off, the powerful emotional bond between two romantically involved partners starts to build up. The lessons of relationship and pair-bonding that our primordial ancestors learnt are deeply encoded in our modern brains as neurological circuits of love. They are present from the moment we're born and activated at puberty by the cocktail of neurochemicals. It's an elegant synchronized system.

At first our brain weighs a potential partner, and if the person fits our ancestral wish-list, we get a spike in the release of chemicals that makes us dizzy with a rush of unavoidable infatuation. It's the first step down the road that leads to pair-bonding. And it is this bond, that defines the true merit of a relationship. Moreover, it is the truest form of love that you can experience in a relationship, and it is not definable by any fake image of beauty in the media.

Hence, this true love is independent of all dogmas and delusions. This true love is independent of all prejudices. This true love is independent of all objectifications. But the most crucial thing to know about true love is that, it is not something you can find, rather you need to build it with the person in whose eyes you see your soul.

CHAPTER 4

Women & Religion

Ours is a patriarchal society, and hence, it is no wonder, that the most scriptures of this society quite gloriously depict men as the authority figures in the world, and women as their subordinate, nay, slaves really. That's how the scriptures have been created, to glorify patriarchy and promote misogyny. All of these scriptures were made by men – none of them came from some Supreme Almighty Being. All the messages of the scriptures which are most respectfully embraced by the human population as divine revelations, were exclusive constructions of ordinary human brains, mostly in a state of transcendence.

These so-called Instruction Manuals have nothing to do with any kind of Supreme Creator whatsoever, even if there is one. Every single word of the scriptures, be it good or bad, was born inside the human brain, from the little wisps of protoplasm. Not a single word of the holy texts came from any celestial source. All those sacred words were constructed by humans in order to suit the personal needs of the humans. Now the question that I'd like to ask is, what's the point of having so many sophisticated scriptures and highly venerated prophets if they do not possess the simple ability to teach us plain ordinary everyday kindness for the human self, regardless of the illusory gender barrier! In what way are they "holy", if they consistently belittle the women and empower the men! If this is holiness, then I am afraid it is of no use to the human society. Any text that neglects the women has not the slightest clue of what holiness really is.

Neglect of women is the major cause for the society's downfall. The man and the woman are the two wheels of the society. If either one becomes defective, the society cannot make progress. There will be hope for the well-being of the entire world only if the humans, men and women alike, stop deeming the women as some kind of inferior creatures.

It is extremely unfortunate that only a few of the world religions put woman in the same pedestal as the man. And the major religious scriptures of the world, such as those of Judaism, Hinduism and Islam are downright monstrous on this matter, since they are filled with unambiguous misogynic verses made by their compilers. To talk about gender-equality in religion, the most important figure that comes to my mind is Siddhartha Gautama. In the gracious eyes of this great awakened human being, so named Buddha, gender did not exist in religion. To him, gender was of complete irrelevance to religion.

The glorious character of Buddha shines like a radiant sun with nothing but deepest human kindness and respect for all of humanity. He was a simple person who lived a simple monastic life and was totally incapable of being a heartless misogynist. The very core of Buddha's philosophical teachings is based upon boundless kindness and compassion towards all beings. In many cases Buddha advised the householders about the roles and status of the two genders which must have stood out in his culture for the reciprocity and mutual respect he recommended. Take the following verse from one of the Buddhist scriptures, Digha Nikaya for instance, where he described the respective duties of husbands and wives.

Digha Nikaya 31

"In five ways should a wife as Western quarter, be ministered to by her husband: by respect, by courtesy, by faithfulness, by handing over authority to her, by providing her with ornaments. In these five ways does the wife minister to by her husband as the Western quarter, love him: her duties are well-performed by hospitality to kin of both, by faithfulness, by watching over the goods he brings and by skill and industry in discharging all business."

And almost five hundred years later another man walked in his footsteps towards diminishing primitive fundamentalism and patriarchal authoritarianism. He was Jesus of Nazareth.

In this context, I can't help but bring up a few verses from the Quran and the Hadith, supposedly provided by Mohammed as advice to the householders.

Sahih Al-Bukhari 7:62:122

"Narrated Abu Huraira:

The Prophet said, "If a woman spends the night deserting her husband's bed (does not sleep with him), then the angels send their curses on her till she comes back (to her husband).""

Quran, Surah 4 (An-Nisa), Ayat 34

"Men are in charge of women by [right of] what Allah has given one over the other and what they spend [for maintenance] from their wealth. So righteous women are devoutly obedient, guarding in [the husband's] absence what Allah would have them guard. But those [wives] from whom you fear arrogance - [first] advise them; [then if they persist], forsake them in bed; and [finally], strike them. But if they obey you [once more], seek no means against them. Indeed, Allah is ever Exalted and Grand."

I shall not go into the theological debate about how much misogynic Mohammed was, or whether he was a man of peace or violence. Because as I have said countless times, the human self is fusion of good and evil. All you need to do is embrace the good and discard the evil. Even a toddler can tell that, those words were simply the product of a man's (could be Mohammed or the later compilers of those scriptures) own mind playing tricks in order to satisfy his deepest and darkest desires. So, his desires took the form of sacred command, when he was having what we may call "the divine experience of a lifetime". It is not really his fault that he and most prophets perceived such self-created messages as coming from a supernatural entity, since during an altered state of consciousness such as in divine transcendence, it is almost impossible for any human being to tell the right from the wrong, and the good from the bad.

One's personality influences those sacred messages received in transcendence to a large extent. After all, Mohammed, Buddha, Christ and all other prophets of humankind were simple humans. But what they learnt in their altered state of mind are distinctively different from each other, due to their own unique personalities, urges, beliefs and fantasies. A human being has both good and bad elements in his or her personality. Biologically we are predisposed to be either bad or good at times, based on the need of the circumstances. It is all inside our head.

The limbic system of our brain, holds all our deepest and darkest secrets. It is the house of our kinkiest desires. This wild feature of the human mind is what we may call the "Id", in psychoanalytic terms. "Id" is the wild beast within each one of us. This beast is reckless and beyond all social norms. This drives our innate evolutionary instinct of surviving even in the harshest climate. Because, nature doesn't give a damn about any living creature. She exists and will keep on existing, with or without us. It is us who needs nature, not the other way around. For this exact reason, in primitive days humans had to fight hard in the wild environment of Mother Nature, against all calamities. And this age-old fight for survival has molded the human brain only as per the parameters of survival. Whatever we are today, is a product of millions of years long constant battle for survival. Nature selects biological features as well as destroys them when deemed unnecessary.

In the harsh climate of the wild, the limbic system may have been our best bet for survival, but as we started to understand our uniqueness, things began to change. We understood the power of community. We realized that, together we could fight even the fiercest predators, but alone we'd be simply their prey. Naturally, Mother Nature put selective pressure on the human brain to evolve substantially, making it go through complex neural reorganization while increasing in size to a great extent then decreasing a little.

Human brain is the organ of unparalleled importance. It is the mother organ that drives every single mechanism in the body. It is the organ with which you see, perceive, observe, think, reminiscence, pleasure and even carry out feats of spiritual or mystical significance such as sensing an incomprehensible supernatural air in the world, giving it a comprehensible form through language and ultimately creating the scriptures while depicting the source of those scriptures in some Supreme Invisible Entity.

Essentially, the evolution of the human brain has been one of the most significant events in the evolution of hominin life. It has been a 6 million years long mosaic process of size increase laced with episodes of reorganization of the cerebral cortex. And the human brain is the most intricate, complicated and impressive organ ever to have evolved on planet earth. The most obvious evolutionary change during human evolution has been the increase in size and complexity of the human brain.

The study of the evolution of human brain is an intriguing domain of scientific exploration. It's like talking to the ghosts of our extinct ancestors through their fossil remnants. This is what we call "Paleoneurology". Paleoneurology allows us to look into the details of brain structure of extinct species through close observation of endocasts (endocranial casts). It is a subfield of paleoanthropology. Paleoanthropological studies show us that social organization was imperative for the early hominins to survive in the harsh environment. So, natural selection forced the brain to develop primitive social interaction through gesture and mimicry. Such selective natural pressure gave our early Australopithecine ancestors cortical capacity for social coordination. Also, any negative emotional outbreak would attract the attention of the predators, so our early ancestors had to develop emotional control. As the early humans gained control over their emotions by the augmentation of the prefrontal cortex, their social communities became more stable. This is exactly when our ancestors took the first step towards being civilized humans from wild beasts.

This was all because of the augmentation in the frontal lobes, especially the prefrontal cortex. The prefrontal cortex (PFC) is the brain region that keeps the primitive beast within the limbic system from lashing out.

- ### *Biopsy of Religions: Neuroanalysis towards Universal Tolerance*

In usual waking state of consciousness, the PFC decides which emotion at what intensity should be expressed depending on the situation. It is through the cortical gateway of the PFC that the limbic emotions find their way out into the environment through behavior. Various factors are involved in this mechanism, including social norms and the common distinction between right and wrong. Analyzing all the internal and external data available to the mind, the PFC makes its final decision. Let me bring up an excerpt that depicts the neurological mechanism of decision-making, from my book "What is Mind?".

Given a situation, where you need to make a decision, the prefrontal cortex (PFC) of your brain, first analyzes all the options available to you while accessing the correlated implicit and explicit memory of your past experiences. Then in context of a set of needs and your personal history, the PFC potentiates the neural pathway for the execution of the most preferable among all the possible options.

Various regions of the prefrontal cortex are involved in distinctive cognitive and behavioral operations. And the regions that are specifically involved in various aspects of decision-making are - ventromedial prefrontal cortex (vmPFC), dorsolateral prefrontal cortex (dlPFC) and orbitofrontal cortex (OFC).

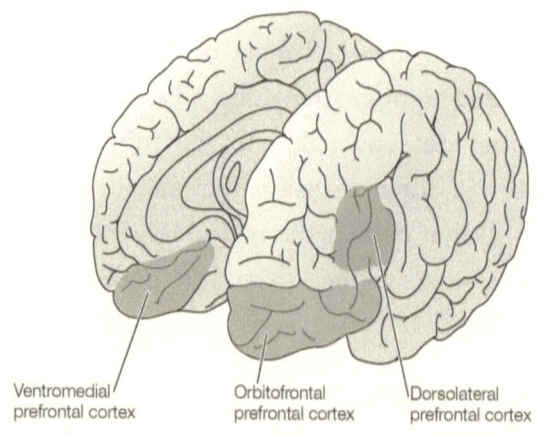

Ventromedial
prefrontal cortex

Orbitofrontal
prefrontal cortex

Dorsolateral
prefrontal cortex

Figure 4.1 Prefrontal regions involved in decision-making

The vmPFC is crucial for your freedom of will to make a decision. Patients with bilateral lesions in the vmPFC develop severe impairment in personal and social decision-making, even though most other intellectual mental abilities remain intact. Damage to this region (especially in the right hemisphere) also leads to mental deficit in detecting irony, sarcasm and deception. People with damaged vmPFC are prone to be easily influenced by misleading advertising, due to their lack of doubt and skepticism.

The ventromedial prefrontal cortex is connected to and receives input from the ventral tegmental area, amygdala, the temporal lobe, the olfactory system, and the dorsomedial thalamus. It, in turn, sends signals to many different brain regions including, the temporal lobe, the amygdala, the lateral hypothalamus, the hippocampal formation, the cingulate cortex, and certain other regions of the prefrontal cortex. This huge network of connections affords the vmPFC the ability to receive and monitor large amounts of sensory data and thereafter influence your decision-making ability.

Emotions are a significant part of our mental lives. And vmPFC plays a key role in regulating emotions and inhibiting them if necessary, by influencing the limbic system, particularly the amygdala. The neural circuitry of the vmPFC is the birthplace of the moral nature of your behaviors and beliefs. Hence, malfunction in this region of your brain, cripples the very element of your mental morality. Without the healthy activity of the vmPFC individuals endorse actions of self-preservation that often break moral values associated with the term human, and inflict harm to others. And the most glaring instance of such vmPFC deficit can be seen in the phenomenon of religious terrorism, or more commonly jihad.

On the other hand, another crucial brain region involved in decision-making is dorsolateral prefrontal cortex (dlPFC). It manages various cognitive functions of the mind, such as working memory, cognitive flexibility, and planning. And when it comes to decision-making, dlPFC carries out all the risky stuff. When given several options to choose from, the dlPFC evokes the mental preference towards the most reasonable option while suppressing temptation in order to maximize personal gain. It gives birth to the ability of self-control in a certain situation for a better outcome. Unlike the vmPFC which makes decisions based upon moral values, healthy activity in the dlPFC facilitates self-preservation. In particular it plays three distinct roles in your mental life:

1. *provides cognitive control to override predominant social-emotional responses elicited by the dilemmas,*
2. *facilitates abstract reasoning, such as, cost-benefit analyses, and*
3. *generates self-centered and other-aversive emotions such as, anger, frustration, or moral disgust.*

Also, quite fascinatingly, several studies have shown that, increased activity of the dlPFC is often associated with psychopathic traits.

Thus, both the vmPFC and dlPFC are intertwined at a functional level along with another prefrontal region called the orbitofrontal cortex, when it comes to make a decision. Increased activity of the dlPFC without the correlated functions of the vmPFC leads to apparently inhuman and antisocial traits of psychopathy. On the other hand, without the healthy activity of the dlPFC, you would probably start to show altruistic attitude. Thus, in order to sustain a healthy life, dlPFC and vmPFC keep each other in check. In fact, when the both are working in proper harmony, you'd have excellent self-control as well as fantastically effective moral values, that would ultimately enrich your mental life. In simple terms, moral values are encoded in your vmPFC, and effective selfishness is encoded in your dlPFC. And you need both, in order to survive.

Orbitofrontal cortex also plays a significant role in decision-making. It enables you to anticipate the possible reward or punishment in a certain situation. It signals the expected rewards/punishments of an action given the particular details of a situation. In doing this, the brain is capable of comparing the expected reward/punishment with the actual delivery of reward/punishment, thus, making the OFC critical for adaptive learning. Thus, OFC plays the part in your mental life, where it analyses the potential emotional outcome of a certain decision in a specific situation.

This way, every single decision of your life is predicated on the healthy functioning of the prefrontal cortex. Even a slight malfunction in a tiny chunk of neuron anywhere in the PFC would lead to the mental deficit in your logical decision-making.

- ## What is Mind?

For a person with a lucid state of consciousness, the PFC weighs all the available options in minute detail before making a decision or judgement. But when the consciousness itself goes into a state of transcendence, all the sociological factors influencing your decision and judgement vanish. In this state, the human mind is biologically incapable of perceiving any kind of social norms and even the simplest distinction between right and wrong, or civilized and barbaric. In this state of consciousness, an individual's true personality finds its way out. Hence, a nomadic personality gives rise to a scripture that is filled with nomadic instincts of imperialism. A misogynic personality constructs a scripture filled with depictions of inferiority of women. Whereas decent and gentle personalities develop exquisite philosophical teachings of kindness, love, compassion and reasoning.

The point is, as long as divinity resides within the human heart as an abstract sentiment, peace and harmony prevail. But the moment, humans try to express this sentiment in words, it is destined to have substantial impact over the society. Now it is up to you, whether you choose the good elements of those textual teachings, or simply gobble everything that is in there, good and bad elements alike, thus halting the progress of humanity. In order to elucidate on this matter, I shall bring up some unambiguous verses from the Islamic, Jewish and Hindu scriptures. I shall not comment on whether they consist of elements of true humanity or plain primitive madness. Any modern human being with a functioning conscience can make the judgement.

Sunan Abu Dawud 11:2142, 2155

"Mohammed said: A man will not be asked as to why he beat his wife.

Mohammed said: If one of you marries a woman or buys a slave, he should say: "O Allah, I ask You for the good in her, and in the disposition You have given her; I take refuge in You from the evil in her, and in the disposition You have given her." When he buys a camel, he should take hold of the top of its hump and say the same kind of thing."

Quran, Surah 2 (Al-Baqarah), Ayat 282

"O you who have believed, when you contract a debt for a specified term, write it down. And let a scribe write [it] between you in justice. Let no scribe refuse to write as Allah has taught him. So let him write and let the one who has the obligation dictate. And let him fear Allah , his Lord, and not leave anything out of it. But if the one who has the obligation is of limited understanding or weak or unable to dictate himself, then let his guardian dictate in justice. And bring to witness two witnesses from among your men. And if there are not two men [available], then a man and two women from those whom you accept as witnesses - so that if one of the women errs, then the other can remind

her. And let not the witnesses refuse when they are called upon. And do not be [too] weary to write it, whether it is small or large, for its [specified] term. That is more just in the sight of Allah and stronger as evidence and more likely to prevent doubt between you, except when it is an immediate transaction which you conduct among yourselves. For [then] there is no blame upon you if you do not write it. And take witnesses when you conclude a contract. Let no scribe be harmed or any witness. For if you do so, indeed, it is [grave] disobedience in you. And fear Allah . And Allah teaches you. And Allah is Knowing of all things."

Sahih Al-Bukhari 1:6:301

"While on his way to pray, Mohammed passed a group of women and he said, "Ladies, give to charities and donate money to the unfortunate, because I have witnessed that most of the people in Hell are women.

They asked, "Why is that?"

He answered, "You swear too much, and you show no gratitude to your husbands. I have never come across anyone more lacking in intelligence, or ignorant of their religion than women. A careful and intelligent man could be misled by many of you."

They responded, "What exactly are we lacking in intelligence or faith?"

Mohammed said, "Is it not true that the testimony of one man is the equal to the testimony of two women?"

After they affirmed that this was true, Mohammed said, "That illustrates that women are lacking in intelligence. Is it not also true that women may not pray nor fast during their menstrual cycle?" They said that this was also true.

Mohammed then said, "That illustrates that women are lacking in their religion.""

Sahih Muslim 17:4206

"There came to Mohammed a woman who said: Allah's Messenger, I have committed adultery, [...] When she was delivered she came with the child (wrapped) in a rag and said: Here is the

child whom I have given birth to. He said: Go away and suckle him until you wean him. When she had weaned him, she came to him with the child who was holding a piece of bread in his hand. She said: Allah's Apostle, here is he as I have weaned him and he eats food. He entrusted the child to one of the Muslims and then pronounced punishment. And she was put in a ditch up to her chest and he commanded people and they stoned her."

Sahih Al-Bukhari 7:62:124

"Narrated Usama:

The Prophet said, "I stood at the gate of Paradise and saw that the majority of the people who entered it were the poor, while the wealthy were stopped at the gate (for the accounts). But the companions of the Fire were ordered to be taken to the Fire. Then I stood at the gate of the Fire and saw that the majority of those who entered it were women.""

Sahih Muslim 3:0684

"Abu Musa then said, "When is a bath obligatory?" Aisha responded, "You have asked

the right person. Mohammed has said that a bath is obligatory when a man is en- compassed by a woman and their circumcised genitalia touch.""

The Old Testament, Genesis 2:21-23

"And the LORD God caused a deep sleep to fall upon Adam, and he slept: and he took one of his ribs, and closed up the flesh instead thereof And the rib, which the LORD God had taken from man, made he a woman, and brought her unto the man. And Adam said, This is now bone of my bones, and flesh of my flesh: she shall be called Woman, because she was taken out of Man."

The Old Testament, Exodus 20:17

"Thou shalt not covet thy neighbour's house, thou shalt not covet thy neighbour's wife, nor his manservant, nor his maidservant, nor his ox, nor his ass, nor any thing that is thy neighbour's."

The Old Testament, Exodus 21:7-11

"And if a man sell his daughter to be a maidservant, she shall not go out as the menservants do. If she please not her master, who hath betrothed her to himself, then shall he let her be redeemed: to sell her unto a strange nation he shall have no power, seeing he hath dealt deceitfully with her. And if he have betrothed her unto his son, he shall deal with her after the manner of daughters. If he take him another wife; her food, her raiment, and her duty of marriage, shall he not diminish. And if he do not these three unto her, then shall she go out free without money."

The Old Testament, Leviticus 21:7,9

"They shall not take a wife that is a whore, or profane; neither shall they take a woman put away from her husband: for he is holy unto his God.

And the daughter of any priest, if she profane herself by playing the whore, she profaneth her father: she shall be burnt with fire."

The Old Testament, Numbers 1:2

"Take ye the sum of all the congregation of the children of Israel, after their families, by the house of their fathers, with the number of their names, every male by their polls."

The Old Testament, Numbers 30:1-16

"And Moses spake unto the heads of the tribes concerning the children of Israel, saying, This is the thing which the LORD hath commanded. If a man vow a vow unto the LORD, or swear an oath to bind his soul with a bond; he shall not break his word, he shall do according to all that proceedeth out of his mouth. If a woman also vow a vow unto the LORD, and bind herself by a bond, being in her father's house in her youth; And her father hear her vow, and her bond wherewith she hath bound her soul, and her father shall hold his peace at her: then all her vows shall stand, and every bond wherewith she hath bound her soul shall stand. But if her father disallow her in the day that he heareth; not any of her vows, or of her bonds wherewith she hath bound her soul, shall stand: and the LORD shall forgive her, because her father disallowed her. And if she had at all an husband, when she

vowed, or uttered ought out of her lips,
wherewith she bound her soul; And her husband
heard it, and held his peace at her in the day that
he heard it: then her vows shall stand, and her
bonds wherewith she bound her soul shall stand.
But if her husband disallowed her on the day
that he heard it; then he shall make her vow
which she vowed, and that which she uttered
with her lips, wherewith she bound her soul, of
none effect: and the LORD shall forgive her. But
every vow of a widow, and of her that is
divorced, wherewith they have bound their
souls, shall stand against her. And if she vowed
in her husband's house, or bound her soul by a
bond with an oath; And her husband heard it,
and held his peace at her, and disallowed her not:
then all her vows shall stand, and every bond
wherewith she bound her soul shall stand. But if
her husband hath utterly made them void on the
day he heard them; then whatsoever proceeded
out of her lips concerning her vows, or
concerning the bond of her soul, shall not stand:
her husband hath made them void; and the
LORD shall forgive her. Every vow, and every
binding oath to afflict the soul, her husband may

establish it, or her husband may make it void. But if her husband altogether hold his peace at her from day to day; then he establisheth all her vows, or all her bonds, which are upon her: he confirmeth them, because he held his peace at her in the day that he heard them. But if he shall any ways make them void after that he hath heard them; then he shall bear her iniquity. These are the statutes, which the LORD commanded Moses, between a man and his wife, between the father and his daughter, being yet in her youth in her father's house."

The Old Testament, Deuteronomy 24:1

"When a man hath taken a wife, and married her, and it come to pass that she find no favour in his eyes, because he hath found some uncleanness in her: then let him write her a bill of divorcement, and give it in her hand, and send her out of his house."

Manusmriti VIII:1 (one of the many Hindu scriptures)

"If a wife, proud of the greatness of her relatives or (her own) excellence, violates the duty which

she owes to her lord, the king shall cause her to be devoured by dogs in a place frequented by many."

Manusmriti IX:1-3

"I will now propound the eternal laws for a husband and his wife who keep to the path of duty, whether they be united or separated.

Day and night woman must be kept in dependence by the males (of) their (families), and, if they attach themselves to sensual enjoyments, they must be kept under one's control.

Her father protects (her) in childhood, her husband protects (her) in youth, and her sons protect (her) in old age; a woman is never fit for independence."

Manusmriti IX:17

"(When creating them) Manu allotted to women (a love of their) bed, (of their) seat and (of) ornament, impure desires, wrath, dishonesty, malice, and bad conduct."

Manusmriti IX:72

"Though (a man) may have accepted a damsel in due form, he may abandon (her if she be) blemished, diseased, or deflowered, and (if she have been) given with fraud."

Vishnusmriti XXV:14

"After the death of her husband, to preserve her chastity, or to ascend the pile after him."

If we look closely into the sacred texts of what we call "Hinduism", we would discover that they quite boastfully consider all women as born promiscuous. In a later part of the Hindu epic Mahabharata there is a whole section where the guardian figure Bhishma, while lying on a bed of arrows, explains to Yudhisthira the innate qualities of women by reciting a conversation between the celestial Sage Narada and the Apsara Panchachuda.

Mahabharata, Anusasana Parava, Section XXXVIII (one of the two major Hindu epics, the other being Ramayana)

"Yudhishthira said, 'O best of the Bharatas, I wish to hear thee discourse on the disposition of

women. Women are said to be the root of all evil. They are all regarded as exceedingly frail.'

Bhishma said, 'In this connection is cited the old history of the discourse between the celestial Rishi Narada and the (celestial) courtezanPanchachuda. Once in ancient times, the celestial Rishi Narada, having roamed over all the world, met the ApsaraPanchachuda of faultless beauty, having her abode in the region of Brahman. Beholding the Apsara every limb of whose body was endued with great beauty, the ascetic addressed her, saying, 'O thou of slender waist, I have a doubt in my mind. Do thou explain it.'

Bhishma continued, 'Thus addressed by the Rishi, the Apsara said unto him, 'If the subject is one which is known to me and if thou thinkest me competent to speak on it, I shall certainly say what is in my mind.'

Narada said, 'O amiable one, I shall not certainly appoint thee to any task that is beyond thy competence. O thou of beautiful face, I wish to hear from thee of the disposition of women.'

Bhishma continued, 'Hearing these words of the celestial Rishi, that foremost of Apsaras replied unto him, saying, 'I am unable, being myself a woman, to speak ill of women. Thou knowest what women are and with what nature they are endued. It behoveth thee not, O celestial Rishi, to set me to such a task.' Unto her the celestial Rishi said, 'It is very true, O thou of slender waist! One incurs fault by speaking what is untrue. In saying, however, what is true, there can be no fault.' Thus addressed by him, the Apsara Panchachuda of sweet smiles consented to answer Narada's question. She then addressed herself to mention what the true and eternal faults of women are!'

Panchachuda said, 'Even if high-born and endued with beauty and possessed of protectors, women wish to transgress the restraints assigned to them. This fault truly stains them, O Narada! There is nothing else that is more sinful than women. Verily, women, are the root of all faults. That is, certainly known to thee, O Narada! Women, even when possessed of husbands having fame and wealth, of handsome features and completely obedient to them, are prepared to disregard them if they get the opportunity. This, O puissant one, is a sinful disposition with us women that, casting off modesty, we cultivate the companionship of men of sinful habits and intentions. Women betray a liking for those men who court them, who approach their presence, and who respectfully serve them to even a slight extent. Through want of solicitation by persons of the other sex, or fear of relatives, women, who are naturally impatient of all restraints, do not transgress those that have been ordained for them, and remain by the side of their husbands. There is none whom they are incapable of admitting to their favours. They never take into consideration the age of the person they are prepared to favour. Ugly or handsome, if only the person happens to belong to the opposite sex, women are ready to enjoy his companionship. That women remain faithful to their lords is due not to their fear of sin, nor to compassion, nor to wealth, nor to the affection that springs up in their hearts for kinsmen and children. Women living in the bosom of respectable families envy the condition of those members of their sex that are young and well-adorned with jewels and gems and that lead a free life. Even those women that are loved by their husbands and treated with great respect, are seen to bestow their favours upon men that are hump-backed, that are blind, that are idiots, or that are dwarfs. Women may be seen to like the companionship of even those men that are destitute of the power of locomotion or those men that are endued with great ugliness of features.

O great Rishi, there is no man in this world whom women may regard as unfit for companionship. Through inability to obtain persons of the opposite sex, or fear of relatives, or fear of death and imprisonment, women remain, of themselves, within the restraints prescribed for them. They are exceedingly restless, for they always hanker after new companions. In consequence of their nature being unintelligible, they are incapable of being kept in obedience by affectionate treatment. Their disposition is such that they are incapable of being restrained when bent upon transgression. Verily, women are like the words uttered by the wise.

Fire is never satiated with fuel. Ocean can never be filled with the waters that rivers bring unto him. The Destroyer is never satiated with slaying even all living creatures. Similarly, women are never satiated with men. This, O celestial Rishi is another mystery connected with women. As soon as they see a man of handsome and charming features, unfailing signs of desire appear on their persons. They never show sufficient regard for even such husbands as accomplish all their wishes, as always do what is agreeable to them and as protect them from want and danger. Women never regard so highly even articles of enjoyment in abundance or ornaments or other possessions of an agreeable kind as they do the companionship of persons of the opposite sex. The destroyer, the deity of wind, death, the nether legions, the equine mouth that roves through the ocean, vomiting ceaseless flames of fire, the sharpness of the razor, virulent poison, the snake, and Fire--all these exist in a state of union in women. That eternal Brahman whence the five great elements have sprung into existence, whence the Creator Brahma hath ordained the universe, and whence, indeed, men have sprung, verily from the same eternal source have women sprung into existence. At that time, again, O Narada, when women were created, these faults that I have enumerated were planted in them!'"

Atharva Veda 6:XI

"Asvattha on the Sami-tree. There a male birth is certified. There is the finding of a son: this bring we to the women-folk.

The father sows the genial seed, the woman tends and fosters it. This is the finding of a son: thus hath Prajapati declared.

Prajapati, Anumati, Sinivali have ordered it. Elsewhere may he effect the birth of maids, but here prepare a boy."

Atharva Veda 14:I

"A wife is given by God to a husband to serve him and to bear him children. Further she is referred to by her husband as his subordinate and slave"

Rig Veda 10:XCV:15

"Nay, do not die, Pururavas, nor vanish: let not the evil-omened wolves devour thee. With women there can be no lasting friendship: hearts of hyenas are the hearts of women."

Such is the glory of the sacred texts, that are supposed to serve humanity in its path of progress. The point is, no text, being human creation, is free from flaws – it is the human mind that should be conscientious enough to accept their good elements and discard the bad ones.

The true essence of religion lies in the human mind, not in any book. In the domain of true religion, mere book-learning has no right to enter. Religion doesn't mean obeying some textual rules from books that were written hundreds or thousands of years ago. Religion means realization of the self. It means feeling the divinity within you. If it doesn't come naturally, then it's not religion, it's just textual fanaticism, which only leads to chaos in the scientifically advanced modern world.

There is an apparent conflict between the terms *Science* and *Religion*, because of people's misperception of religion. To people religion is often perceived as a book. And from this very misperception rises all kinds of kinds of social conflicts surrounding the term "religion". Hence, these conflicts are not really caused by religion, rather by the stupidity of people, who consider scriptures and religions to be synonymous.

If to a person religion means reading books and obeying every single word from it without the slightest bit of reasoning, then such perception would only bring destruction upon the person and the world. Also, there are people who use the words from those books to justify their own filthy actions. Let's take a conservative Muslim, for example. Say, this conservative Muslim male creature is found to be beating his wife. Now, if someone says to him *"this is wrong"*, he would abruptly reply, *"this is a divine thing to do, my book says so"*. Now, if a Christian says *"my book is older, so you should stop obeying your book and start obeying mine"*, there will come the Buddhist, and say, *"my book is much older still, obey mine"*. Then will come the Jew, and say, "my *book is even older, so just follow mine"*. And in the end will come the Hindu and say *"my books are the oldest of all, obey them"*. Therefore, referring to books will only make a mess of the human race and tear the species into pieces.

I say to you again, religion is not a book. All the current dilemma of the human society whether a specific religion (supposedly Islam) *is a religion of peace or of violence,* is founded upon the belief that a religion is a specific book. But the reality is not so simple. Religion is a natural feature of the human mind that created all the scriptures in the world, not the other way around. Religion is the mind's urge to become better in the spiritual domain. All those books only depict that urge. They only show what a handful of individuals in the history of mankind experienced when their brain made them transcend from an ordinary wakeful state into an ultimate state of divinity and bliss. Thus, all divinity, spirituality and religiosity exist within your very brain.

Hence, the book from which to learn religion is the book of your own mind. The fundamentalists are often ignorant about the true beauty of divinity, because they read the wrong books. Your religion is whatever makes you a better human being. Your religion is whatever enables you to see the pain of another fellow creature. Your religion is whatever gives you the power to loosen the knots of prejudices in the human society. In short, every act of kindness is religion, whereas every act of hatred is blasphemy.

Religion doesn't divide the human society. The humans reading the wrong books to understand religion, do. Religion is to be realized, not only heard. It is not in learning some doctrines and regurgitating them like a parrot. The human mind has been endowed by Mother Nature through the process of selective pressure, with unbelievable qualities. And one of those qualities is divinity. Divinity rises from the very neurons inside your head. No book on this planet can give you the description of terms like *religion, spirituality, divinity* unless you discover it within the realm of your own mind.

As I have said in "In Search of Divinity",

In this modern world, religion often faces loads of criticism mainly from the scientific community because of the absurdity that goes along with it. It is because, religion is not taught as a science of experience, instead, it is only instructed in the institutions as a matter of memorizing some doctrines and obeying them without any doubt. This is sole cause behind the rise of the illusory battle between Science and Religion. The moment, religious preachers around the world start teaching religion from experience, rather than from books, the perceptual gap between the scientific mind and the religious mind would slowly start to fade away.

Self-realization is the truest essence of religion. Realize your true nature. That is all there is to do. Know yourself as you are – particles of start-dust moving through the eternal ocean of time, trying to make whatever little difference you can. That is practical religion. That is the religion of thinking humanity. That is scientific religion. Everything else is impractical, for everything else will perish.

The pursuit of excellence – that's the purpose of the human species on this planet. And this excellence doesn't come by obeying doctrines. Excellence comes through rigorous efforts of rectifying the flaws in the doctrines and making them more advanced to suit the human pursuit of the development.

Science proceeds in exactly this manner, through constantly questioning and analyzing the predominant scientific laws and modifying them if necessary. If science, as the most advanced tool in the hands of rational humanity can have the guts to change itself based on the needs of the time and society, why can't religion as the most influential tool in the hands of divine humanity, modify itself?

Science and Religion are two vividly different realms of the human mind. They work differently at the molecular level, but the purpose of both is alleviation of the Mind from the darkness of ignorance. Hence, only a fool would attempt to destroy one to ensure the survival of the other. For a truly fascinating and healthy future of humanity, these two distinct faculties of the human mind must assimilate the goodness of each other. One shall enrich the other, in the ultimate pursuit of the truth.

Through the newly emerged field of Neurotheology, Scientists such as Andrew Newberg, Michael Persinger, myself and a few others have already taken the first step from the side of Science, to diminish the gap between Science and Religion. Now it is time for Religion to do the same. And the moment any religion does that, the eternal battle between Science and Religion would slowly start to disperse. Buddhism did this long ago. Christianity has already started to make sincere efforts. And now it's time for the rest of the religions to do the same, especially Judaism, Hinduism and Islam.

And the first step towards making this possible is to cease the blind faith upon bookish ideas of religion. Religion must be realized, not taught or learnt. And the greatest religion is, to be true to your own nature. Discover that nature and nourish it with all your heart and soul. If you do not exist as your true self, how can God exist!

God and all of its associated divinity exist through you – through your mind.

The existence of true religion is predicated on the practice of goodness. Goodness is Godliness. There is nothing else. Religion lies in practice, not in theories. If you go to a church and memorize the phrase *love thy neighbor,* then keep repeating it to every single person you meet, it doesn't make you religious. In this specific scenario, you'd be called truly religious, or truly Christian, if and only if you practice that motto in your personal life and actually start deeming your neighbor as your own beloved family member.

There is no Science in the world that can deny such an act of compassion and brotherhood. This is possible only because the scientific mind of humanity is not rigid, it is flexible. It can bend towards any direction that ultimately tends to do good to humanity. Religion must learn the same. And the moment any religion learns that, it would become the most scientific religion in the world.

Theoretical religion being based upon heartless indoctrination has already made a mess of our human society. Now is the time for the current perception of religion to evolve. Now is the time for scientific religion to rise. Religion is a natural phenomenon of the human mind, but today, in the hands of theoretical bloodsucking religious preachers it has become a lifeless mockery. Now is the time that you take back religion from those intellectual idiots and place it where it belongs, in the temple of your inner cosmos.

God is the experience that gave rise to all the scriptures, yet it is not tied to any of them. God is like the H2O in a lake. Some drink it at one place and call it "water", others at another place and call it "jal", and some others at a third place and call it "pani". The Christians call it "water", the Hindus "jal", and the Muslims "pani". But it is one and the same thing. As the different streams having their sources in different places all mingle their water in the sea, the different paths which humans take through different tendencies, various though they appear, crooked or straight, all lead to the same Absolute

Oneness. That Oneness or God, is not tied to the doctrines of any church, synagogue, temple or mosque, yet it is the reason of their birth.

A rational human being of the civilized world would be like the swan that can draw the milk from a mixture of milk and water, leaving aside the water. He or she would be like an ant that can take the sugar from a mixture of sugar and sand, leaving aside the sand. Take the elements of goodness that appeal to you from all the religions and ignore the rest. Feel the divinity in everything you do. Discover religion in your own way. Unfold your own inner mysteries.

Nature gave us the neural elements of divinity, and we made Gods and religions out of them. Nature gave us variations in melanin level, and we made races out of them. Nature gave us lands, we made national borders out of them. So far, every single boon that we have received from Nature, has been used more in the act of building barriers among ourselves than in the process of unification. We fight over religion, we fight over race, we fight over language, we fight over castes and creeds. I ask you my friend, how long will we keep on fighting with our own kind? I ask you, O conscientious soldier, how long will it take for you to take action?

A truly civilized person with a scientific religion in heart, is psychologically incapable of nourishing any idea of separatism. A rational mind of the modern world would know that, all religions are simply many paths leading to the same domain of transcendental bliss, while a theoretical book-learned creature from the medieval times would never embrace this simple fact an hence, build barriers of beliefs. That's all the difference there is between scientific religion and theoretical religion.

Scientific religion is compatible with modern Science, and in fact, they enrich each other. They smoothen each other's path of progress. While on the contrary, far from being compatible with Science, theoretical religion consistently tries to impede the development of human society, with primordial evils such as misogyny, polygamy and homophobia. Thus, it relentlessly keeps making efforts to drag the human society back to the Stone Age.

I am afraid, if we don't act now, the day is not far, that this beautiful planet of ours, which we call home, shall be turned into a dry barren wasteland by the advocates of theoretical religion. In a relentless battle of mostly the men to prove the greatness and authority of one religion over the others, there would be no humans left to impose the theories on. In the end, all that will remain are books, covered with blood, but no human being to read them. Is this the future you want for your children? Is this the world you are going to offer your off-springs?

If not, then you need to start working right now. Start working on your child's mind. Start building your child's character. Raise your child as a human being, instead of raising boys and girls. Raise human beings with the religion of love in their hearts. Raise human beings with the language of compassion on their lips. Raise human beings with the color of joy on their face. Raise human beings with the force of bravery in their nerves. And these brave conscientious souls with the flames of compassion in their hearts shall one day change the course of human history. They shall build a world where humans will be defined by the purity of character, instead of the barbarian measures of gender, race or religion. They - shall build a genuine abode of peace. They – shall become the true wise species on earth. And it all starts with you.

CHAPTER 5
Women & Society

Why does a woman not feel comfortable under her own skin? Why is she not satisfied with her own body? What can there possibly be not to like about your own self. Remember, the Self is the measure of everything. You don't need to see yourself through the delusional eyes of the society. It's the society that needs to see you, through your eyes. And this happens, only when you start to respect yourself, beyond all the perceptual limitations of the society. It is only when you are confident about your own self, that the society begins to hail you the way you want.

Why do you give a damn about what the society thinks of you! Why do you compare yourself with the delusion perfection running rampant on TV and computer screens! Why do you let the society judge you based on that false image of beauty and perfection! Build your own standard my friend. Build your own measure of perfection.

I'd rather listen to what you think of yourself, than what the whole world has to say about you. It is you, who has to define your image, not the society. It is you, who has to define your character, not the society. It is you who has to define your identity, not the society. I believe in you my friend, so much so, that if any of my ideas make you feel belittled in any manner, I want you to rise against me and throw my work into the fire. Any notion, any book, any institution that weakens the self instead of strengthening it, must be discarded at ones.

The only quality that can resolve the current sociological crisis of gender discrimination is strength of character in all women. Endow yourself with the strength of the Bengal tigress, and the society shall have no other choice but to accept you as equal of men. Remember, the society hails those as weak who hail themselves as weak, and those as strong who hail themselves as strong. Your strength of character shall define the fate of the whole womankind, nay, the whole of humankind.

The first principle of humanism in the "Principia Humanitas", says "Self is All". It means that the Self is the measure of everything. If the ocean is so beautiful and surreal, it is so in the subjective reality of the Self. If the night sky is so soothing and calm, it is so because the Self perceives it as such. If your romantic partner is so handsome or beautiful, it is so in the individualistic reality of your Self. All systems of the society, be it religious, cultural, educational or anything else, are meant to serve the Self, not the Self to serve the systems. No God, no religion, no race, no gender is greater than the Human Self. And this my friend, is the core principle of being a human.

Truth in the human world, is constructed, defined and then reconstructed by the human self. Truth independent of the human self is irrelevant to human existence. Thus, every truth in this human world is a Human Truth, not the Ultimate Truth. The reality as we know or perceive by the faculties of the Self, is a Human Reality, for it is a mere simulation in the neurons of the human brain. And as such, that reality may have some traces of the actual reality, but, in the end, it is a humanly relevant reality, not the Reality, which is independent of the Human Self. Hence, every single human perception in the world is a human construction. And perceptions never remain constant – they keep evolving. This gives you the opportunity to make the sociological perception of womanhood evolve. It is all in your hands, O Brave Human!

Humanity shall not have the existential right to call itself "Sapiens" (wise) until it bestows on its every member equal rights in every aspect of life. To be called sapiens, they must act as sapiens. To be called wise, they must act as wise. To be the most advanced species on earth, they must behave as such, not just in the sophisticated domain of soulless technology, but in the domain of sentiments – in the domain of conscience. Being wise does not mean being able to build nuclear weapons - it means, being able to build nuclear weapons and yet to know when to destroy them for the greater good. Being wise means being aware of your own forte as well as recognize the forte of another person. Being wise means judging another person, if necessary, not based on race, religion or gender, but based on his or her character.

All sorts of misogyny and gender discriminations thrive on lack of vigor in character. Once your character is poured with vigor and your attitude radiates confidence, there is no power in any external force to have any form of authority over you. Nothing in the universe can have power over you, until you foolishly lose independence at your own will. Due to the lack of self-awareness, the mind puts itself in a position of slavery of external forces. And it is only the mind that can free itself from all slavery. Set the mind free my friend, and it will find its own salvation! Set the Self free, and it will attain its own independence! Liberty of thought and the courage to act upon it, are the core principles of human existence – these are the principles of growth and wellbeing. Become self-aware my friend! That's all you need, to proceed in the path of gender mutuality – in the path of genuine progress. As you become aware of your truest self, you will slowly come to learn that nothing in the universe is more powerful than your inner self.

You are surrounded by ignorance, savagery and fanaticism. You live in a society where everyone thinks he or she knows about everything in the whole universe. If you find yourself among those intellectual idiots, then being good and humble may only give rise to self-doubts. So, you must learn to distinguish between real and shallow intellect. Then, as a self-preservation tactic, you need to let your pretence of arrogance grow as big as a Dinosaur, so that the fake intellectuals start to realize their true inferiority in front of you. To shed some more light on this matter, let me tell you a story.

Once upon a time, some shepherd boys used to tend their sheeps in a meadow where a dreadful poisonous snake lived. Everyone was afraid of it. One day a saint was going along the meadow. The boys ran to him and said: *"Revered sir, please don't go that way. A venomous snake lives over there."*

"What of it, my good children?" said the saint. *"I am not afraid of the snake. I know some hymns that will keep the snake away."*

Saying this, he continued on his way along the meadow. But the shepherds, being afraid, did not accompany him. In the meantime the snake moved swiftly toward him with upraised hood. As soon as it came near, he recited a hymn, and the snake somehow lied down at his feet like an earthworm.

The saint said: *"Look here. Why do you go about doing harm? Come, I will give you a holy word. By repeating it you will learn to love God. Ultimately you will realize Him and so get rid of your violent nature."*

Saying this, he taught the snake a holy mumbo-jumbo word and initiated it into spiritual life. The snake bowed before the teacher and said, *"Revered sir, how shall I practice spiritual discipline?"*

"Repeat that sacred word", said the teacher, *"and do no harm to anybody"*. As he was about to depart, the saint said, *"I shall see you again."*

Some days passed and the shepherds noticed that the snake would not bite. They threw stones at it. Still it showed no anger. It behaved as if it were an earthworm. One day one of the boys came close to it, caught it by the tail, and, whirling it round and round, dashed it again and again on the ground and threw it away. The snake threw up blood and blacked out. It was half-dead. It could not move. So, thinking it dead, the boys went their way.

Late at night the snake regained consciousness. Slowly and with great difficulty it dragged itself into its hole. It could hardly move. Many days passed. The snake became a mere skeleton covered with a skin. Now and then, at night, it would come out in search of food. For fear of the shepherds it would not leave its hole during the day-time. Since receiving the sacred word from the teacher, it had given up doing harm to others. It maintained its life on dirt, leaves, or the fruit that dropped from the trees.

About a year later the saint came that way again and asked about the snake. The shepherds told him that it was dead. But he couldn't believe them. He found his way to the place and, searching here and there, called it by the name he had given it. Hearing the teacher's voice, it came out of its hole and bowed before him with great reverence.

"How are you?" asked the saint. *"I am well, sir"*, replied the snake. *"But"*, the teacher asked, *"why are you so thin?"* The snake replied: *"Revered sir, you ordered me not to harm anybody. So I have been eating only leaves and fruit. Perhaps that has made me thinner."*

The snake had developed the quality of humility. It could not be angry with anyone. It had totally forgotten that the shepherds had almost killed it.

The saint said: *"It can't be mere want of food that has reduced you to this state. There must be some other reason. Think a little."* Then the snake remembered that the boys had dashed it against the ground. It said: *"Yes, revered sir, now I remember. The boys one day dashed me violently against the ground. They are ignorant, after all. They didn't realize what a great change had come over my mind. How could they know I wouldn't bite or harm anyone?"*

The saint exclaimed *"What a shame! You are such a fool! You don't know how to protect yourself. I asked you not to bite, but I didn't forbid you to hiss. Why didn't you scare them away by hissing?"*

Putting aside the hogwash of snake-charming, the point of the whole story is that you must hiss at people who intend to undermine your individuality with their false pride and intellectual stupidity. You must frighten them away, lest they should do you harm. Act like you have a lot of venom inside you, but never inject them into anyone.

Be excellent in your own terms. Do not look for approval from a single soul on this planet, man or woman. Respect yourself and in time the whole world will respect you. Do not become self-absorbed, but become self-aware. Pay attention to the self – listen carefully, and you will discover wonderful answers to the most perplexing questions of life. All the answers that you seek can only be found within. All your sufferings can be alleviated by no other person but you. All the prejudices that you face can only be terminated by you. Every step you take in the path of internal progress, takes the society ten steps forward towards a world free from prejudices and discriminations. Your conscientious footsteps become giant leaps of advancement for whole humanity.

BIBLIOGRAPHY

Abbey, A. (1982). Sex differences in attribution for friendly behavior: Do males misperceive females' friendliness? Journal of Personality and Social Psychology, 42, 830-838.

Abbey, A., McAuslan, P., & Ross, L. T. (1998). Sexual assault perpetration by college men: The role of alcohol, misperception of sexual intent, and sexual beliefs and experiences. Journal of Social and Clinical Psychology, 17, 167-195.

Allen, I. L. (1984). Male sex roles and epithets for ethnic women in American slang. Sex Roles, 11, 43-50.

Allgower, A., Wardle, J., & Steptoe, A. (2001). Depressive symptoms, social support, and personal health behaviors in young men and women. Health Psychology, 20, 223-227.

American Psychological Association. (2007a). Guidelines for psychological practice with girls and women. American Psychologist, 62, 949-979.

Amodio, D.M., & Devine, P.G. (2006). Stereotyping and evaluation in implicit race bias: Evidence for independent constructs and unique effects on behavior. Journal of Personality and Social Psychology, 91, 652-661.

Anton, S. C. Natural history of Homo erectus. American Journal of Physical Anthropology S37, 126-70 (2003)

Antón, S.C., 2003. Natural history of Homo erectus. Yearbook of Physical Anthropology 46, 126–170.

Baars, B. (1988), A Cognitive Theory of Consciousness (New York: Cambridge University Press).

Barbey, A. K., Colom, R., Solomon, J., Krueger, F., Forbes, C., & Grafman, J. (2012). An integrative architecture for general intelligence and executive function revealed by lesion mapping. Brain, 135, 1154–1164.

Barbey, A. K., Grafman, J. in press a. The prefrontal cortex and goal-directed social behavior. In J. Decety & J. Cacioppo (Eds.), The

Handbook of Social Neuroscience. Oxford University Press.

Barbey, A. K., Koenigs, M., & Grafman, J. Dorsolateral prefrontal contributions to human working memory. Cortex, in press b.

Barbey, A. K., & Grafman, J. (2011). An integrative cognitive neuroscience theory for social reasoning and moral judgment. Wiley Interdisciplinary Reviews: Cognitive Science, 2, 55–67.

Basso, A., De Renzi, E., Faglioni, P., Scotti, G., & Spinnler, H. (1973). Neuropsychological evidence for the existence of cerebral areas critical to the performance of intelligence tasks. Brain, 96, 715–728.

Bakan, D. (1966). The duality of human existence. Chicago, IL: Rand McNally.

Balsam, K. F., Rothblum, E. D., & Beauchaine, T. P. (2005). Victimization over the lifespan: A comparison of lesbian, gay, bisexual, and heterosexual siblings, Journal of Consulting and Clinical Psychology, 73, 477-487.

Bartky, S. L. (1990). Femininity and domination: Studies in the phenomenology of oppression. New York, NY: Routledge.

Bearman, S., Korobov, N., & Thorne, A. (2009). The fabric of internalized sexism. Journal of Integrated Social Sciences, 1, 10-47.

Bem, S. (1993). The lenses of gender: Transforming the debate on sexual inequality. New Haven, CT: Yale University Press.

Bettis, P. J., & Adams, N. G. (2003). The power of the preps and a cheerleading equity policy. Sociology of Education, 76, 128-142.

Bordo, S. (1999). The male body: A new look at men in public and in private. New York, NY: Farrar, Straus, & Giroux.

Boyd, C. J. (1996-1997). Smoke and the "F" word: Women and health. Michigan Feminist Studies, 11, 25-37.

Breck, L. R., & Ullman, S. E. (2001). The role of offender alcohol use in rape attacks: An analysis of National Crime Victimization

Survey data. Journal of Interpersonal Violence, 16, 3-21.

Breck, L. R., & Ullman, S. E. (2002). The roles of victim and offender alcohol use in sexual assaults: Results from the National Violence Against Women Survey. Journal of Studies on Alcohol, 63, 57-63.

Breines, J. G., Crocker, J., & Garcia, J. A. (2008). Self-objectification and wellbeing in women's daily lives. Personality and Social Psychology Bulletin, 34, 583-598.

Buchannan, T. S., Fischer, A. R., Tokar, D. M, & Yoder, J. D. (2008). Testing a culture-specific extension of objectification theory regarding African American women's body image. The Counseling Psychologist, 36, 697-718.

Buchannan, T. S., Settles, I. H., & Woods, K. C. (2008). Comparing sexual harassment subtypes among Black and White women by military rank: Double jeopardy, the jezebel, and the cult of true womanhood. Psychology of Women Quarterly, 32, 347-361.

Bureau of Labor Statistics. (2007). Employment by detailed occupation and sex.

Bechara, A., Damasio, A. R., Damasio, H., & Anderson, S. W. (1994). Insensitivity to future consequences following damage to human prefrontal cortex. Cognition, 50, 7–15.

Black, F. W. (1976). Cognitive deficits in patients with unilateral war-related frontal lobe lesions. Journal of Clinical Psychology, 32, 366–372.

Blair, C. (2006). How similar are fluid cognition and general intelligence? A developmental neuroscience perspective on fluid cognition as an aspect of human cognitive ability. Behavioral and Brain Sciences, 29, 109–125.

Blair, R. J. R., & Cipolotti, L. (2000). Impaired social response reversal: a case of "acquired sociopathy". Brain, 123, 1122–1141.

Bugg, J. M., Zook, N. A., DeLosh, E. L., Davalos, D. B., & Davis, H. P. (2006). Age differences in fluid intelligence: contributions of general slowing and frontal decline. Brain and Cognition, 62, 9–16.

Burgess, P. W., & Shallice, T. (1996). Response suppression, initiation and strategy use following frontal lobe lesions. Neuropsychologia, 34, 263–272.

Bear, D.M. (1979), 'Personality changes associated with neurologic lesions', in Textbook of Outpatient Psychiatry, ed. A. Lazare (Baltimore, MD: Williams and Wilkins Co.).

Bogen,J.E.(1995a), 'On the neurophysiology of consciousness: Part I. An overview', Consciousness and Cognition, 4, pp. 52–62.

Bogen, J.E. (1995b), 'On the neurophysiology of consciousness: Part II. Constraining the semantic prob- lem', Consciousness and Cognition, 4, pp. 137–58.

Bickerton, D. (2009). Adam's tongue: How humans made language and how language made humans. New York: Hill and Wang.

Brothers, L. (2002). The social brain: A project for integrating primate behavior and neurophysiology in a new domain. In J. T. Cacioppo et al. (Eds.), Foundations in neuroscience, pp. 367. Cambridge, MA: MIT Press.

Bobe, R., Behrensmeyer, A.K., 2004. The expansion of grassland systems in Africa in relation to mammalian evolution and the origin of the genus Homo. Palaeogeography, Palaeoclimatology, Palaeoecology 207, 399-420.

Bolton, E.B. (1935) 'Effect of knowledge upon attitudes towards the negro', J.Soc.Psy. 6, 68–90.

Boring, E.G. (1942) Sensation and Perception in the History of Experimental Psychology, NY: AppletonCentury-Crofts.

Boring, E.G. (1950 [1929]) A History of Experimental Psychology, 2nd edn, NY: AppletonCenturyCrofts.

Bowler, P. (1983) The Eclipse of Darwinism, Baltimore and London: Johns Hopkins UP.

Boyd, W.C. and Boyd, L.G. (1937) 'Sexual and racial variation in ability to taste phenylthio-carbamide with some data on inheritance', Ann.Eug. 846–51.

Brenman, M. (1940a) 'Minority group membership and religious, psychosexual, and social patterns in a group of middle-class Negro girls',J. Soc.Psy. 12,179–96.

Brenman, M. (1940b) 'The relationship between minority group membership and group identification in a group of urban middle-class Negro girls' , J.Soc.Psy. 11,171–97.

Brenner, A.B. (1948) 'Some psychoanalytic speculations on anti-semitism', The Psychoanalytic Review, 35 (1), 20–32.

Brigham, C.C. (1923) A Study of American Intelligence, Princeton: Princeton UP.

Brinton, D.G. (1902) The Basis of Social Relations. A Study in Ethnic Psychology, NY and London: Albermale.

Brody, N. (1992) Intelligence, 2nd edn, San Diego: Academic Press. Brown, P. (ed.) (1973) Radical Psychology, London: Tavistock.

Brown, R. (1958) Words and Things: An Introduction to Language, NY: Free Press.

Brown, W.O. (1934) 'Culture contact and race conflict', in E.B.Reuter (ed) (1934), 34–37.

Carr, E. R., & Szymanski, D. M. (2011). Sexual objectification and substance abuse in young adult women. The Counseling Psychologist, 39, 39-66.

Chura, H. (2003). Miller set to roll catfight sequels. Advertising Age, 74, 1-35.

Churchland, P.S. (1986), Neurophilosophy (Cambridge, MA: The MIT Press). Churchland, P.S. (1996), 'The hornswoggle problem', Journal of Consciousness Studies, 3 (5–6), pp. 402–8.

Churchland, P.S. & Ramachandran, V.S. (1993), 'Filling in: Why Dennett is wrong', in Dennett and His Critics: Demystifying Mind, ed. B. Dahlbom (Oxford: Blackwell Scientific Press).

Churchland, P.S., Ramachandran, V.S. & Sejnowski, T.J. (1994), 'A critique of pure vision', in Large- scale Neuronal Theories of the Brain, ed. C. Koch & J.L. Davis (Cambridge, MA: The MIT Press).

Cicurel, R., "L'ordinateur ne digérera pas le cerveau", Sarina Editions, 2013

Cobb S., Ramachandran, V.S. & Hirstein, W. (in preparation), 'Evoked potentials during synesthesia'. Cohen, M.S., Kosslyn, S.M., Breiter, H.C. et al. (1996), 'Changes in cortical activity during mental rotation. A mapping study using functional MRI', Brain, 119, pp. 89–100.

Cozolino, L. (2006). The Neuroscience of Human Relationships and the Developing Brain. New York: W.W. Norton & Company.

Cohen, E. (1939) 'Cultural and personality factors in the attitudes of Russian Jewish clients toward relief' , Smith.Coll.Stud.S.W. 10, 151–2.

Conklin, E.G. (1921) The Direction of Human Evolution, NY: Scribner's.

Connolly, J. (1994) 'Of race and right', Irish Times, 6 December.

Cook, S.W. (1957) 'Desegregation: a psychological analysis', Am.Psy. 12,1–13.

Costall, A. (1991) 'Frederic Bartlett and the rise of prehistoric psychology' in A.Still and A.Costa1 : (eds) Against Cognitivism: Alternative Foundations for Cognitive Psychology, Hemel Hempstead: Harvester-Wheatsheaf, 39–54.

Cox, O.C. (1970 [1948]) Caste, Class & Race. A Study in Social Dynamics, NY: Modern Reader.

Crafts, L.W., Schneirla, T.C., Robinson, E.E. and Gilbert, R.W. (eds) (1938) Recent Experiments in Psychology, NY and London: McGraw-Hill.

Crane, A.C. (1923) 'Race differences in inhibition', Arch.Psy. 9, 2–84.

Criswell, J.H. (1939) 'A sociornetric study of race cleavage', Arch.Psy. 235.

Crookshank, F.G. (1931 [1924]) The Mongol in Our Midst. A study of man and his three faces, 3rd edn, London: Kegan Paul, Trench, Trübner.

Cross, W.E. (1991) Shades of Black: Diversity in African American Identity, Madison, WI: University of Wisconsin Press.

Culwick, A.T. and G.M. (1935) 'Religious and economic sanctions in a Bantu tribe', B.J.Psy.26(2), 183–91.

Crick, F. (1994), The Astonishing Hypothesis: The Scientific Search for the Soul (New York: Simon and Schuster). Crick, F. (1996), 'Visual perception: rivalry and consciousness', Nature, 379, pp. 485–6.

Crick, F. & Koch, C. (1992), 'The problem of consciousness', Scientific American, 267, pp. 152–9.

Darwin, Charles. "On the origin of species by means of natural selection" (original edition, 1859).

Darwin, Charles. "The Descent of Man" (original edition, 1871).

Dawkins, R. "The Selfish Gene", Oxford University Press, 1976

Dawkins, R. "The Magic of Reality", Bantam Press, 2011

Davies, S.P. (1930) Social Control of the Mentally Deficient, NY: Thomas Y.Crowell.

Davis, M. and Hughes, A.G. (1927) 'An investigation into the comparative intelligence and attainments of Jewish and non-Jewish schoolchildren', B.J.Psy. 18 (2), 134–46.

Davis, T. M., & Wood, P. S. (1999). Substance abuse and sexual trauma in a female veteran population. Journal of Substance Abuse Treatment, 16, 123-127.

Descamps, M. J., Rothblum, E., Bradford, J., & Ryan, C. (2000). Mental health impact of child sexual abuse, rape, intimate partner violence, and hate crimes in the National Lesbian Health Care Survey. Journal of Gay and Lesbian Social Services, 11, 27-55.

Downs, D. M., James, S., & Cowan, G. (2006). Body objectification, self-esteem, and relationship satisfaction: A comparison of exotic dancers and college women. Sex Roles, 54, 745-752.

Dearborn, W.F. and Long, H.H. (1934) 'The physical and mental abilities of the American negro: a critical survey', JNE 3, 530–47.

Delaney, L. (1972) 'The other bodies in the river', in R.L.Jones (ed.) (1972) 335–43.

Dennis, W. (1940a) 'Does culture appreciably affect patterns of infant behavior?', J.Soc.Psy. 12, 305–17.

Dennett, D.C. (1991), Consciousness Explained (Boston, MA: Little, Brown and Co.).

Devinsky, O., Feldmann, E., Burrowes, K. & Broomfield, E. (1989), 'Autoscopic phenomena with seizures', Archives of Neurology, 46, pp. 1080–8.

DeGiorgio, M. et al. Out of Africa: modern human origins special feature: explaining worldwide patterns of human genetic variation using a coalescent-based serial founder model of migration outward from Africa. PNAS USA 106, 16057-16062 (2009)

Delson, E., Harvati, K., 2006. Return of the last Neanderthal. Nature 443, 762-763.

Driberg, J.H. (1929) The Savage as He Really Is, London: Routledge.

Edelman, G. M. (1992). Bright air, brilliant fire: On the matter of the mind. New York: Basic Books.

Erikson, E.H. (1939) 'Observations on Sioux education', J.Psy. 7, 101–56.

Erikson, E.H. (1950) Childhood and Society, Harmondsworth: Penguin.

Estabrooks, G.H. (1928a) 'The enigma of racial intelligence', J.Genet.Psy. 35, 137–9.

Eugenics Society (1934) 'Aims and Objectives of the Eugenics Society', Eug.Rev. 26.

Evans Pritchard, E.E. (1937) Witchcraft, Oracles and Magic Among the Azande, Oxford: Clarendon Press.

Evarts, A.B. (1916) 'The ontogenetic against the phylogenetic elements in the psychoses of the colored race', Psychoanalytic Review 3, 272–87.

Eysenck, H.J. (1954) Psychology of Politics, London: RKP.

Eysenck, H.J. (1957) Sense and Nonsense in Psychology, Harmondsworth: Penguin.

Eysenck, H.J. (1971) Race, Intelligence and Education, London: Temple Smith.

Eysenck, H.J. vs. Kamin, L. (1981) Intelligence: The Battle for the Mind, London: Pan.

Faludi, S. (1991). Backlash: The undeclared war against American women. New York, NY: Crown.

Fisher, B., Cullen, F., & Turner, M. (2000). The sexual victimization of college women. Washington, DC: U.S. Department of Justice, National Institute of Justice, and Bureau of Justice Statistics.

Fitzgerald, L. F., Drasgow, F., Hulin, C. L., Gefand, M. J., & Magley, V. J. (1997). Antecedents and consequences of sexual harassment in organizations: A test of an integrated model. Journal of Applied Psychology, 82, 578-589.

Frazier, P. A., Tix, A. P., & Barron, K. E. (2004). Testing moderator and mediator effects in counseling psychology research. Journal of Counseling Psychology, 51, 115-134.

Fredrickson, B. L., & Roberts, T. (1997). Objectification theory: Toward understanding women's lived experiences and mental health risks. Psychology of Women Quarterly, 21, 173-206.

Farah, M.J. (1989), 'The neural basis of mental imagery', Trends in Neurosciences, 10, pp. 395–9.

Fiorini, M., Rosa, M.G.P., Gattass, R. & Rocha-Miranda, C.E. (1992), 'Dynamic surrounds of receptive fields in primate striate cortex: A physiological basis', Proceedings of the National Academy of Science 89, pp. 8547–51.

Fodor, J.A. (1975), The Language of Thought (Cambridge, MA: Harvard University Press). Frith, C.D. & Dolan, R.J. (1997), 'Abnormal beliefs: Delusions and memory', Paper presented at the May, 1997, Harvard Conference on Memory and Belief.

Finlay BL, Darlington RB (1995) Linked regularities in the development and evolution of mammalian brains. Science 268:1578–1584

Gazzaniga, M. S. (1985). The social brain. New York: Basic Books. Greenspan, S. I. and S. G. Shanker (2004). The first idea: How symbols, language, and intelligence evolved from our early primate ancestors to modern humans. Cambridge, MA: Da Capo Press.

Gazzaniga, M.S. (1993), 'Brain mechanisms and conscious experience', Ciba Foundation Symposium, 174, pp. 247–57.

Gomberg, E. L. (1996). Women's drinking practices and problems from a lifespan perspective. In J. M. Howard, S. E. Martin, P. D. Mail, M. E. Hilton, & E. D. Taylor (Eds.), Women and alcohol: Issues for prevention research (Research Monograph No. 32, pp. 185-214).

Gordon, M. K. (2008). Media contributions to African American girls' focus on beauty and appearance: Exploring the consequences of sexual objectification. Psychology of Women Quarterly, 32, 245-256.

Greene, B. (1994). African American women. In L. Comas-Diaz & B. Greene (Eds.), Woman of color: Integrating ethnic and gender identities in psychotherapy (pp. 10-29). New York, NY: Guilford.

Gruber, J. E. (1998). The impact of male work environments and organizational policies on women's experiences of sexual harassment. Gender & Society, 12(3), 301-320.

Gutek, B. A. (1985). Sex and the workplace: Impact of sexual behavior and harassment on women, men and organizations. San Francisco, CA: Jossey-Bass.

Gutek, B. A., Cohen, A. G., & Konrad, A. M. (1990). Predicting social-sexual behavior at work: A contact hypothesis. Academy of Management Journal, 33, 560-577.

Gutek, B. A., & Morasch, B. (1982). Sex ratios, sex-role spillover and sexual harassment of women at work. Journal of Social Issues, 38(4), 55-74

Gloor, P., Olivier, A., Quesney, L.F., Andermann, F., Horowitz, S. (1982), 'The role of the limbic system in experiential phenomena of temporal lobe epilepsy', Annals of Neurology, 12, pp. 129–43.

Gloor, P. (1992), 'Amygdala and temporal lobe epilepsy', in The Amygdala: Neurobiological Aspects of Emotion, Memory and Mental Dysfunction, ed J.P. Aggleton (New York: Wiley-Liss).

Goodman M, Grossman LI, Wildman DE (2005) Moving primate genomics beyond the chimpanzee genome. Trends Genet 21:511–517

Goldberg, G., Mayer, N. & Toglis, J.U. (1981), 'Medial frontal cortex and the alien hand sign', Archives of Neurology, 38, pp. 683–6.

Grady, D. (1993), 'The vision thing: Mainly in the brain', Discover, June, pp. 57–66.

Green, R.E. A draft sequence of the Neandertal genome. Science 328, 710-722

Gilbert SL, Dobyns WB, Lahn BT (2005) Genetic links between brain development and brain evolution. Nat Rev Genet 6:581–590

Halgren, E. (1992), 'Emotional neurophysiology of the amygdala within the context of human cognition', in The Amygdala: Neurobiological Aspects of Emotion, Memory and Mental Dysfunction, ed J.P. Aggleton (New York: Wiley-Liss).

Hartley, C.A. & Phelps, E.A. Changing fear: the neurocircuitry of emotion regulation. Neuropsychopharmacology 35, 136–146 (2010).

Horgan, J. (1994), 'Can science explain consciousness?', Scientific American, 271, pp. 88–94.

Humphrey, N. (1993), A History of the Mind (London: Vintage).

Hublin, J.J. The origin of Neanderthals. PNAS 45, 169-177 (2009)

Henshilwood, C.S., Marean, C.W., 2003. The origin of modern human behavior: critique of the models and their test implications. Current Anthropology 44, 627-651.

Hof PR, Nimchinsky EA, Perl DP, Erwin JM (2001) An unusual population of pyramidal neurons in the anterior cingulate cortex of hominids contains the calcium- binding protein calretinin. Neurosci Lett 307:139–142

Hilton, C.E. (Eds) From Biped to Strider: The Emergence of Modern Human Walking, Running, and Resource Transport. Kluwer Academic/Plenum, New York, pp 50-52.

Haeusler, M., McHenry, H., 2004. Body proportions of Homo habilis reviewed. Journal of Human Evolution 46, 433-465.

Hobbs, J. (2006). The origins and evolution of language: A plausible strong-AI account. In M. Arbibi (Ed.), Action to language via the mirror neuron system. Cambridge: Cambridge University Press.

Holloway RL (1996) Evolution of the human brain. In: Lock A, Peters CR (eds) Handbook of human symbolic evolution. Oxford University Press, Oxford, pp 74–114

Horowitz, E.L. (1935) 'A study of the process of the development of attitudes toward negroes', Psy.Bull. 32, 575–6.

Hose, C. and McDougall, W. (1912) The Pagan Tribes of Borneo, a Description of their Physical, Moral, and Intellectual Condition with Some Discussion of their Ethnic Relations, 2 vols, London: Macmillan.

Houts, P.L. (ed.) (1977) The Myth of Measurability, NY: Hart.

Howard, J.H. (1972) 'Toward a social psychology of colonialism', in R.L.Jones (ed.) (1972), 326– 34.

Howe, M. (1988) 'Intelligence as an explanation', B J.Psy. 79 (3), 349–60.

Howitt, D. and Owusu-Bempah, J. (1994) The Racism of Psychology: Time for a Change, Hemel Hempstead: Harvester-Wheatsheaf.

Hughes, A.G. (1928) 'Jews and Gentiles. Their intellectual and temperamental differences', Eug.Rev. 20, 89–97.

Humphrey, S.K. (1917) Mankind: Racial Values and the Racial Prospect, NY: Scribner's.

Hurlock, E.B. (1930) 'The will-temperament of white and negro children', J.Genet.Psy. 38, 91–100.

Huxley, J. and Haddon, A.C. (1935) We Europeans, London: Cape.

Hall, C. C. I., & Crum, M. J. (1994). Women and "body-isms" in television beer commercials. Sex Roles, 31, 329-337.

Hall, E. (1993). Smiling, deferring, and flirting: Doing gender by giving "good service." Work and Occupations, 20, 452-471.

Harper, B., & Tiggemann, M. (2008). The effect of thin ideal media images on women's self-objectification, mood, and body image. Sex Roles, 649-657.

Hebl, L. R., King, E. B., & Lin, J. (2004). The swimsuit becomes us all: Ethnicity, gender, and vulnerability to self-objectification. Personality and Social Psychology Bulletin, 30, 1322-1331.

Henningsen, D. (2004). Flirting with meaning: An examination of miscommunication in flirting interactions. Sex Roles, 50, 481-489.

Hill, M. S., & Fischer, A. R. (2008). Examining objectification theory: Lesbian and heterosexual women's experiences with sexual- and self-objectification. The Counseling Psychologist, 36, 745-777.

Johanson, D.C., White, T.D., Coppens, Y. 1978. A new species of the genus Australopithecus (Primates: Hominidae) from the Pliocene of Eastern Africa. Kirtlandia 28, 2-14.

Jackendoff, R. (1987), Consciousness and the Computational Mind (Cambridge, MA: The MIT Press).

Kanizsa, G. (1979), Organization In Vision (New York: Praeger).

Kanwisher, N., McDermott, J. & Chun, M.M. The fusiform face area: a module in human extrastriate cortex specialized for the perception of faces. J. Neurosci. 17, 4302–4311 (1997).

Kilbourne, J. (1999). Deadly persuasion: Why women and girls must fight the addictive power of advertising. New York, NY: Free Press.

Kilpatrick, D. G., Ruggiero, K. J., Acierno, R., Saunders, B. E., Resnic, H. S., & Best, C. L. (2003). Violence and risk for PTSD, major depression, substance abuse/dependence, and comorbidity: Results from the national survey of adolescents. Journal of Consulting and Clinical Psychology, 71, 692-700.

Klonoff, E. A., Landrine, H., & Campbell, R. (2000). Sexist discrimination may account for well-known gender differences in psychiatric symptoms. Psychology of Women Quarterly, 24, 93-99.

Koss, M. P., Bailey, J. A., Yuan, N. P., Herrera, V. M., & Lichter, E. L. (2003). Depression and PTSD in survivors of male violence: Research and training initiatives to facilitate recovery. Psychology of Women Quarterly, 27, 130-142.

Kozee, H. B., & Tylka, T. L. (2006). A test of objectification theory with lesbian women. Psychology of Women Quarterly, 30, 348-357.

Kozee, H. B., Tylka, T. L., Augustus-Horvath, C. L., & Denchik, A. (2007). Development and psychometric evaluation of the Interpersonal Sexual Objectification Scale. Psychology of Women Quarterly, 31, 176-189.

Kubik, M. Y., Lytle, L. A., Birnbaum, A. S., Murray, D. M., & Perry, C. L. (2003). Prevalence and correlates of depressive symptoms in young adolescents. American Journal of Health Behavior, 27, 546-553.

Kuypers HGJM (1958) Corticobulbar connections to the pons and lower brainstem in man. Brain 81:364–388

Kinsbourne, M. (1995), 'The intralaminar thalamic nucleii', Consciousness and Cognition, 4, pp. 167–71.

Lakoff, G. and M. Johnson (1999). Philosophy in the flesh. Basic Books: New York. LeDoux, J. E. (1996). The emotional brain. New York: Simon & Schuster.

Landrine, H., & Klonoff, E. A. (1997). Discrimination against women: Prevalence, consequences, remedies. Newbury Park, CA: Sage.

Landrine, H., Klonoff, E. A., Alcaraz, R., Scott, J., & Wilkins, P. (1995). Multiple variables in discrimination. In B. Lott & D. Maluso (Eds.), The social psychology of interpersonal discrimination (pp. 193-224). New York, NY: Guilford.

Landrine, H., Klonoff, E. A., Gibbs, J., Manning, V., & Lund, M. (1995). Physical and psychiatric correlates of gender discrimination: An application of the Schedule of Sexist Events. Psychology of Women Quarterly, 19, 473-492.

LaPointe, E. A. (1992). Relationships with waitresses: Gendered social distance in restaurant hierarchies. Qualitative Sociology, 15, 377-393.

Lindberg, S. M., Grabe, S., & Hyde, J. S. (2007). Gender, pubertal development, and peer sexual harassment predict objectified body consciousness in early adolescence. Journal of Research on Adolescence, 17, 723-742.

Lips, H. (1997). Sex and gender: An introduction (3rd ed.). Mountain View, CA: Mayfield.

Luciano, L. (2001). Looking good: Male body image in modern America. New York: Hill & Wang.

Lukas, S. A. (2008). Competition. In The gender ads project.

LeDoux, J.E. (1992), 'Emotion and the amygdala', in The Amygdala: Neurobiological Aspects of Emo- tion, Memory and Mental Dysfunction, ed J.P. Aggleton (New York: Wiley-Liss).

Lieberman, M.D., Hariri, A., Jarcho, J.M., Eisenberger, N.I. & Bookheimer, S.Y. An fMRI investigation of race-related amygdala activity in African-American and Caucasian-American individuals. Nat. Neurosci. 8, 720–722 (2005).

Maryansky, A. (1996). African Ape social structure: A blue print for reconstructing early hominid structure. In J. Steel, S. Sherman (Eds.), The Archeology of Human Ancestry. London: Rutledge.

Massey, D. (2000). What I don't know about my field but wish I did. Annual Review of Sociology, 26(1), 699.

Massey, D. S. (2002). A brief history of human society: The origin and role of emotion in social life: 2001 presidential address. American Sociological Review, 67(1), 1–29.

Miller, B. D. (2007). Cultural anthropology, 4th ed. Boston: Allyn & Bacon.

Mayr, E., 1950. Taxonomic categories of fossil hominids. Cold Spring Harbor Symp Quant Biol 25, 109–118.

Malamuth, N. M., Sockloskie, R. J., Koss, M. P., & Tanaka, J. S. (1991). Characteristics of aggressors against women: Testing a model using a national sample of college students. Journal of Consulting and Clinical Psychology, 59, 670-681.

Martens, M., & Haase, R. (2006). Advanced applications of structural equation modeling in counseling psychology research. The Counseling Psychologist, 34, 878-911.

Martens, M. P., Rocha, T. L., Martin, J. L., & Serrao, H. F. (2008). Drinking motives and college students: Further examination of a four-factor model. Journal of Counseling Psychology, 55, 289-295.

McCaul, M. E., & Svikis, D. S. (1999). Intervention issues for women. In J. P. Ott, R. E. Tarter, & R. T. Ammerman (Eds.), Sourcebook on substance abuse: Etiology, epidemiology, assessment, and treatment (pp. 430-439). Boston, MA: Allyn & Bacon.

McCreary, D. R., & Sasse, D. K. (2000). An exploration of the drive for muscularity in adolescent boys and girls. Journal of American College Health, 48, 297-320.

McKinley, N. M., & Hyde, J. S. (1996). The Objectified Body Consciousness Scale: Development and validation. Psychology of Women Quarterly, 20, 181-215.

Mercurio, A. E., & Landry, L. J. (2008). Self-objectification and well-being: The impact of self-objectification on women's overall sense of self-worth and life satisfaction. Sex Roles, 58, 458-466.

Meyer, I. H. (2003). Prejudice, social stress, and mental health in lesbian, gay, and bisexual populations: Conceptual issues and research evidence. Psychological Bulletin, 129, 674-697.

Martinez, I., Rosa, L., Arsuaga, J.-L. Jarabo, P., Quam, R., Lorenzo, C., Gracia, A., Carretero, J.-M., Bermúdez de Castro, J.M., Carbonell, E., 2004. Auditory capacities in Middle Pleistocene humans from the Sierra de Atapuerca in Spain. Proceedings of the National Academy of Sciences 101, 9976-9981.

MacDonald, A.W., Cohen, J.D., Stenger, V.A. & Carter, C.S. Dissociating the role of the dorsolateral prefrontal and anterior cingulate cortex in cognitive control. Science 288, 1835–1838 (2000)

MacLean, P.D. (1990), The Triune Brain in Evolution (New York: Plenum Press).

MacKay, D.M. (1969), Information, Mechanism and Meaning (Cambridge, MA: The MIT Press).

Marr, D. (1982), Vision (San Francisco: Freeman). Medawar, P. (1969), Induction and Intuition in Scientific Thought (London: Methuen).

Milner, A.D. & Goodale, M.A. (1995), The Visual Brain In Action (Oxford: Oxford University Press).

Nagel, T. (1974), 'What is it like to be a bat?', Philosophical Review, 83, pp. 435–50.

Nash, M. (1995), 'Glimpses of the mind', Time, pp. 44–52.

Naskar, Abhijit. (2015). "Love Sutra: The Neuroscientific Manual of Love"

Naskar, Abhijit. (2016). "Biopsy of Religions: Neuroanalysis towards Universal Tolerance"

Naskar, Abhijit. (2016), "What is Mind?"

Naskar, Abhijit. (2016), "In Search of Divinity: Journey to The Kingdom of Conscience"

Naskar, Abhijit. (2017), "The Education Decree"

Naskar, Abhijit. (2017), "Principia Humanitas"

Naskar, Abhijit. (2017), "We Are All Black: A Treatise on Racism"

Nicolelis, M. & Cicurel, R., "The Relativistic Brain: How it works and why it cannot be simulated by a Turing machine", Kioss Press, 2015

Nielson, J.M. & Jacobs, L.L. (1951), 'Bilateral lesions of the anterior cingulate gyri', Bulletin of the Los Angeles Neurological Society, 16, pp. 231–4.

Nimchinsky EA, Gilissen E, Allman JM, Perl DP, Erwin JM and Hof PR (1999) A neuronal morphologic type unique to humans and great apes. Proc Natl Acad Sci USA 96:5268–5273

Novembre, J., J. K. Pritchard and G. Coop (2007). Adaptive drool in the gene pool. Nature Genetics, 39, 1188.

O'Donnell, J.M. (1985) The Origins of Behaviorism: American Psychology, 1870–1920, NY and London: NYUP.

Penfield, W.P. & Perot, P. (1963), 'The brain's record of auditory and visual experience: a final summary and discussion', Brain, 86, pp. 595–696.

Penrose, R. (1994), Shadows of the Mind (Oxford: Oxford University Press).

Penrose, R. (1989), The Emperor's New Mind: Concerning Computers, Minds and The Laws of Physics (Oxford: Oxford University Press).

Phelps, E.A., Cannistraci, C.J. & Cunningham, W.A. Intact performance on an indirect measure of race bias following amygdala damage. Neuropsychologia 41, 203–208 (2003).

Plum, F. & Posner, J.B. (1980), The Diagnosis of Stupor and Coma (Philadelphia: F.A. Davis and Co.).

Posner, M.I. & Raichle, M.E. (1994), Frames of Mind (New York: Scientific American Library).

Preuss TM, Caceres M, Oldham MC, Geschwind DH (2004) Human brain evolution: insights from microarrays. Nat Rev Genet 5:850–860

Purpura K.P. & Schiff, N.D. (1997), 'The thalamic intralaminar nuclei: a role in visual awareness', The Neuroscientist, 3, pp. 8–15.

Ramachandran, V.S. (1993), 'Filling in gaps in logic: Some comments on Dennett', Consciousness and Cognition, 2, pp. 165–8.

Ramachandran,V.S.(1995a),'Filling in gaps in logic: Reply to Durginetal.', Perception, 24,pp.41-845.

Ramachandran, V.S. and Blakeslee, S. (1999), Phantoms in the Brain: Probing the Mysteries of the Human Mind (William Morrow Paperbacks)

Richmond, B.G., Jungers, W.L., 2008. Orrorin tugenensis femoral morphology and the evolution of hominin bipedalism. Science 319, 1662-1665.

Rilling JK Human and nonhuman primate brains: are they allometrically scaled versions of the same design? Evol Anthropol 15:65–77

Relethford, J. H. Genetic evidence and the modern human origins debate. Heredity 100, 555-563 (2008)

Roebroeks, W. & P. Villa. On the earliest evidence for habitual use of fire in Europe. PNAS USA Epub ahead of print (2011)

Rossion, B., Schiltz, C. & Crommelinck, M. The functionally defined right occipital and fusiform face areas discriminate novel from visually familiar face. Neuroimage 19, 877–883 (2003).

Roth, G. and Dicke, U. Evolution of the brain and intelligence, TRENDS in Cognitive Sciences Vol. 9, No. 5, 2005

Rightmire, G.P., 1998. Human evolution in the Middle Pleistocene: the role of Homo heidelbergensis. Evolutionary Anthropology 6, 218-227.

Searle, John R. (1980), 'Minds, brains, and programs', Behavioral and Brain Sciences, 3, pp. 417–58.

Searle, John R. (1992), The Rediscovery of the Mind (Cambridge, MA: The MIT Press).

Semendeferi K, Lu A, Schenker N, Damasio H (2002) Humans and great apes share a large frontal cortex. Nat Neurosci 5:272–276

Strauss, E., Risser, A. & Jones, M.W. (1982), 'Fear responses in patients with epilepsy', Archives of Neu- rology, 39, pp. 626–30.

Sherwood CC, Broadfield DC,Gannon PJ,Holloway RL, Hof PR (2003) Variability of Brocas area homologue in African great apes: implications for language evolution. Anat Rec 71A:276–285

Smith, C.E. (1934) 'A new approach to the problem of racial differences', JNE 3, 523–9

Spoor, F., Leakey, M.G., Gathogo, P.N., Brown, F.H., Antón, S.C., McDougall, I., Kiarie, C. Manthi, F.K, Leakey, L.N., 2007. Implications of new early Homo fossils from Ileret, east of Lake Turkana, Kenya. Nature 448, 688–691.

Stringer, C.B., Finlayson, J.C., Barton, R.N.E, Fernández-Jalvo, Y., Cáceres, I., Sabin, R.C., Rhodes, E.J., Currant, A.P., Rodríguez-Vidal, J., Giles-Pacheco, F., Riquelme-Cantal, J.A., 2008. Neanderthal exploitation of marine mammals in Gibraltar. Proceedings of the National Academy of Sciences USA 105, 14319–14324.

Shipman, P., 2008. Separating "us" from "them": Neanderthal and modern human behavior. Proceedings of the National Academy of Sciences USA 105, 14241-14242.

Schmitt, D., Churchill, S., 2003. Experimental evidence concerning spear use in Neandertals and early modern humans. Journal of Archaeological Science 30, 103-114.

Sutherland, N.S. (1989), The International Dictionary of Psychology (New York: Continuum).

Sawer, G. and Deak, V. (2007). The last human (p. 103). New York: Peter N. Nevraumont Publication – Yale University Press.

Small, D. (2008). On the deep history of the brain. Berkeley: University of California Press.

Turner, B. (2000a). Embodied ethnography. Doing culture. Social Anthropology, 8(1), 51.

Turner, J. H. (2000b). On the origins of human emotions: A sociological inquiry into the evolution of human affect. Stanford, California: Stanford University Press.

Tovee, M.J., Rolls, E.T. & Ramachandran, V.S. (1996), 'Rapid visual learning in neurones of the primate temporal visual cortex', Neuroreport, 7, pp. 2757–60.

Trinkhaus, E., 1985. Pathology and the posture of the La Chappelle-aux-Saints Neanderthal. American Journal of Physical Anthropology 67, 19-41.

Trinkaus, E., Shipman, P., 1993. The Neanderthals: Changing the Image of Mankind. Knopf: New York.

Thorpe, S.K.S., Holder, R.L., Crompton, R.H., 2007. Origin of human bipedalism as an adaptation for locomotion on flexible branches. Science 316, 1328-1331.

Terre et des planètes / Earth and Planetary Sciences 332, 137-144 (2001)

Ungar, P.S., Grine, F.E., Teaford, M.F., 2006. Diet in early Homo: a review of the evidence and a new model of adaptive versatility. Annual Review of Anthropology 35, 209-228.

Waxman, S.G. & Geschwind, N. (1975), 'The interictal behavior syndrome of temporal lobe epilepsy', Archives of General Psychiatry, 32, pp. 1580-6.

Ward, C. V. et al. Complete fourth metatarsal and arches in the foot of Australopithecus afarensis. Science 331, 750-753 (2011)

Ward, C. V. Interpreting the posture and locomotion of Australopithecus afarensis: where do we stand? American Journal of Physical Anthropology S35, 185-215 (2002)

White, T. D. et al. Ardipithecus ramidus and the paleobiology of early hominids. Science 326, 75-86 (2009)

Woodworth, R.S. (1916) 'Comparative psychology of races', Psy.Bull. 13, 388–96.

Woodworth, R.S. (1918) Dynamic Psychology. The Jessup Lectures 1916–1917, NY: Columbia UP.

Woodworth, R.S. (1946, 18th edn) Psychology. A Study of Mental Life, London: Methuen

Wray,A.(1998)."Protolanguage as a holistic system for social interaction," Language & Communication 18, pp. 47–67.

Young, N. M. et al. The phylogenetic position of Morotopithecus. Journal of Human Evolution 46, 163-184 (2004)

Zeki, S.M. (1978), 'Functional specialisation in the visual cortex of the rhesus monkey', Nature, 274, pp. 423–8.

Zeki, S.M. (1993), A Vision of the Brain (Oxford: Oxford University Press).

ABHIJIT NASKAR

www.ingramcontent.com/pod-product-compliance
Lightning Source LLC
Chambersburg PA
CBHW020508290526
45786CB00002B/523